CLASSROOM Remixed

Incorporating
Technology
in the
Globalized Classroom

**JEREMY RINKEL
MAJHON PHILLIPS**

Classroom Remixed:
Incorporating Technology in the Globalized Classroom
Copyright © 2010 by Globalize Our Generation, Inc.
All rights reserved.

ISBN-13: 978-0-9844270-0-0
ISBN-10: 0-9844270-0-7

Published by Globalize Our Generation, Inc.
Printed in the United States of America.
Printed by CreateSpace, LLC

www.globalizeourgeneration.com

Dedicated to all educators who remain lifelong learners, all teachers and mentors who strive unceasingly to make lifelong positive changes in the lives of their students.

Table Of Contents

Introduction...1

Section I:
Students of Today.................................7

Chapter 1: Brief Introduction to the Millennials...9
Chapter 2: An In-Depth Look At Students.........19

Section II:
The Problems Surrounding U.S. Schools......47

Chapter 3: Fostering Cosmopolitanism............49
Chapter 4: Pitfalls to Testing.........................65

Section III:
Using Technology in the Classroom............83

Chapter 5: Creating a Globalized Classroom....85
Chapter 6: The Digital Classroom...................97
Chapter 7: Tools for Students.......................111
Chapter 8: Tools for Teachers......................125

Section IV:
The Future of Education..........................137

Chapter 9: Teaching Individuality..................139
Chapter 10: The Promise of OERs...............157

Appendixes..171

INTRODUCTION

Critical Changes for a Standardized World

Our world is rapidly changing.

Our children are losing their ability to think critically and creatively.

The public school system is holding teachers accountable for standardized test scores and federal funding.

Through this standardization our students are losing their individuality.

The loss of individuality leads to students not valuing their education.

With this attitude, how can we expect to reach these students? Furthermore, how can we help them live in their increasingly "global" world?

Educators need to adopt different methodologies of teaching to reach today's students.
Through open educational resources (OERs) and other new and affordable technologies, educators have the opportunity to foster a creative-thinking, problem solving individual, not just another factory-produced high school graduate.

    As educators, both of us understand the difficulties of teaching in our modern age. Even if used for just an hour a day, there are tools to involve your students in the global world and technology that can make a big difference.

Digital communication is easily accessible and functional. To prove our point we wrote this book and collaborated edits with absolutely no physical or face-to-face meetings. All communication was accomplished via online tools like Skype, Elluminate, WizIQ, e-mail, and wikis.

Education in the U.S. needs not only to be evaluated, but also desperately needs reform. We are concerned that as a country, our students are not ready for the global world. National policy is slow and difficult to change, so instead we focus on little things that can make a positive difference in your classroom and the lives of your students.

As our chapters came together, we noticed four different sections or themes. Through these pages we will explore, who our students are (Section 1), what is being lost in United States schools (Section 2), what technology exists to help educators (Section 3), and the future of education with a focus on open education (Section 4).

Section 1 will focus on the question: Who are the students today? These chapters explore who fits into the millennial generation and why this age group is different from generations of the past. Our students are the first native digital generation. They cannot receive information the same way older generations did. They require fast-paced knowledge structures and interactive lesson planning.

In Section 2, we will discuss what is being lost in America's schools. We explore the notion of creating a globalized classroom and the importance of creativity and critical thinking skills. We will also look into the increase of standardization and how it affects students' individuality. The final chapter of this section looks at the pitfalls of standardized testing and NCLB mentality. We will also suggest ways to foster Cosmopolitan ideals in a rigid educational structure.

In Section 3, our focus shifts to technology and how it is helpful to educators. These chapters have practical examples on how to create a digital and global classroom, how to find and use technological tools for students and teachers, and how to apply technology on a tight budget. Oftentimes these tools can be found relatively inexpensive or even free.

In Section 4, we explore the future of education. Looking at the issue of inequality within public schools, we suggest a variety of open educational resources that can transform your teaching and classroom. We aim to help your students become citizens of the global world.

Through our own use of these ideas, we feel that the chapters of this book provide relevant academic research and practical ideas for the global educator at home and in the classroom.

SECTION I

Students of Today

Chapter 1

Brief Introduction to the Millennial Generation

American Millennials are likely to have a huge impact on the population of the whole world-

Eric Greenburg (Generation WE)

Millennials are children or young adults who were born between the years of 1978 and 2002. This generation is known as the first "native digitals." Since childhood, Millennials have used computers, mobile phones, mp3 players, and electronics. In the classroom, Millennials are generally considered selfish, aloof, and needy for acknowledgement. Likewise, they often appear to be lazy, in demand of instant gratification, and self-involved in the workplace. Why is this generation so different from generations in the past? Will the world change to cater to the new generation of citizens and workers? Or, will this generation eventually "mature"?

Kids In the War-Zone

Lawrence Grossberg (2005) thinks that kids today are in a war-zone due to zero-tolerance in the community and schools, media's portrayal of their disobedient and dangerous behavior, and their parents' blame game of entertainment, technology, and capitalism. He infers that today's youths are considered "the Other" in modern society; a new breed of human that no one can explain.

On a 60-Minutes special in May 2008, Morley Safer interviewed consultants, executives, and young professionals. Safer repeatedly mentioned the notion of Millennials needing praise, with the blame going back to their childhoods. The parents of this generation told each and every one of them that they were special. Rarely did the children have to accomplish or do anything for the praise they were given, they simply had to exist. Therefore, as workers and students, they believe they deserve recognition for merely showing up. The accusatory tone of this story continues, by including phrases such as:

1. "A new breed of worker is about to attack everything you hold sacred."
2. From teaching them how to cover their tattoos to "how to eat with a fork and knife."
3. The Millennial generation is happy to live at home with their parents. "Who couldn't be happy living in a world without failure?"

The Millennials are shown to be immature, irresponsible, hopelessly self-centered, and nearly useless. The final point made by Morley Safer, is that Millennials need further nurturing and time to mature. The workforce waits, anxiously, for the Millennial generation to grow into adulthood. Hopefully they will reach maturity around age 30 (Textor, 2008).

The Spoiled Generation

Millennials are children who know that they are wanted. The use of birth control methods skyrocketed during the late seventies, eighties, and nineties. The typical Millennial childhood is based around schedules, confidence building activities, team-oriented efforts, and technology. ("Understanding," 2009). Attacks such as Columbine and 9/11 created a nation of terrified parents, and their children became extremely sheltered as security in the communities, schools, and neighborhoods heightened. Due to this security, Millennial children are not allowed to play in the neighborhood parks alone; therefore socializing is a part of their "in-home" lives on the Internet. Instant Messaging, virtual reality games, and social networking sites have become a vital part of this generation's existence.

Schools and classrooms are often considered a bore to this multi-tasking generation. At home, these students can easily listen to music, instant message, surf the net, do homework, and talk on the phone simultaneously. At school, they are forced to sit quietly in their desks, watching the blackboard and listening to a single lecture. Even the computer in the classroom and the teacher's knowledge of technology is backdated compared to their at-home learning environment.

Diana Oblinger (2003) claims that the Millennial generation insists on prompt customer service, 24/7 amenities, constant communication, and no technological delays. She states also that their learning styles are tremendously different than those of previous generations, "[a]long with differences in attitudes, Millennials exhibit distinct learning styles. For example, their learning preferences tend toward teamwork, experiential activities, structure, and the use of technology. Their strengths include multitasking, goal orientation, positive attitudes, and a collaborative style."

Scholars and researchers have a few disagreements regarding the Millennials. In "Understanding Millennials" (2009), this generation is labeled as non-creative and conservative:

> Millennials have also been accused of being a generation of followers, willing to be led and accepting rules and restrictions more easily than the generations before them. Because of this, many educators have noticed a lack of willingness to take risks and step "outside the box" in their schoolwork. As a whole, they are less concerned with standing out or being creative and more concerned with fitting in and doing what is expected of them.

However, one of the few positives mentioned in 60- Minutes' "The Millennials are Coming" (Textor, 2008) was that Millennials can bring a lot of creativity, and creative energy into the work place.

What is the working definition of creativity? Millennials are probably not as artistic as the Boomers or Gen X with their appearance, attire, and décor, yet does this mean they are not creative? They do tend to follow rules, due to the lack of tolerance for disobedience, but does that mean that they have lost the ability to think freely? Many computer programmers, network creators, and website designers stem from this generation. Perhaps Millennials have lost the physical aspect of creativity, but creative thinking is self-evident through their work with multi-media projects, P2P collaborations, and technological structure building. I argue that creativity is not lost, simply transformed into a different, and perhaps even more advanced form.

Generation WE- And Positives of the Trans-National Millennial Student Body

According to Greenberg and Weber (2009), Millennials are a trans-national generation. American Millennials believe that they have more in common with their own generation around the developed world, than they do with older generations in their own nation. As the first digital generation, these youths communicate daily with other peers internationally due to social networking sites, games, and instant messaging. They have also traveled extensively, in and out of their home country. Greenberg and Weber believe that this is the first trans-national generation. Imagine literally having the world at your fingertips from the time of birth. These children do not know any national boundaries or extreme nationalism. Greenberg and Weber (2009) also claim that Millennials are quite philanthropic, and that they are interested in new energies, and ultimately desire positive changes in their world.

This generation requests a lot more out of their teachers, parents, and bosses than previous generations did. However, their technical knowledge, critical thinking, and sheer youth can be a positive addition to the school and workplace. Although cynical, Millennials are positive about the future of their country and the world. They are firm believers that when they are the majority of the nation's demographic, positive changes can and will be made.

Adapting to this Generation in the Classroom

A question often posed by educators who frequently work with the Millennial generation is, "How will the use of technology in education change the identities and behaviors of the Millennial generation?" I truly believe that there are two possible outcomes. The first is in direct reference to Nicholas Carr (2008), and his work, "Is Google Making Us Stupid?" Students in these online settings, with personalized programs, will neglect their work for play, discipline will be completely lost, and we will breed a generation of youths who cannot learn. On the other hand, with such interesting and valuable resources available online, could students find education interesting? For once in history, will personalized education be thought of as "play" rather than "work?"

It truly depends on how these programs are presented. If educators can embrace the multi-media opportunities of online education, and are willing to accept "fun" ideas such as avatars, personalized programs, Internet identities, and creativity, we may begin to see a new approach to learning from both teachers and students.

Another problem with the Millennial generation is that they are rarely satisfied. They want new technologies, new information, and fast-paced learning. Their learning styles are much like the technology they use so often. They want a change every three months, when the newest and latest computer is offered on the market. However, as educators, we realize that our budgets and school budgets simply cannot afford such luxuries. We do not have the capabilities to purchase new computers three times a year, nor do we have the time to stay ahead in our own training of the technologies being offered.

There are a few options for classroom teachers to keep Millennials interested and understanding of their environment in the classroom. First, educators should seek to keep them involved. Communicate with them as equals (their parents do, you should too), allow them to create ideas based on your lesson plans ("next week we will be discussing the Gold Rush, would anyone like to help decorate the classroom or create ideas on how to cover this topic?"), and allow them to use multi-media resources to accomplish a task (creating a multi-media collaboration can be a lot more exciting for you and them than having them write a research paper).

    The educator may never know as much about the technology as their students. However, through collaboration between the students and the teacher, quality learning can be achieved.

Chapter 2

An In-Depth Look at Students Today

Youth Culture: The New "Other"

Generation Y is entitled, lazy, selfish, tech savvy, and incompetent-

Scott Greenfield

The Millennial generation has been given many names ranging from Generation Y, to Generation WE, to a continuation of Generation ME. There are some things, however, that most agree upon when looking at this generation. This generation was born around the turn of the Millennium, somewhere between 1978 and 2002. They are the catered generation of primarily financially secure baby boomers. Millennials were the first native digital generation. Parents and students of this generation saw, and continue to see, education as a commodity-- they are the consumers and they want it done their way. Due to their technical knowledge and vast education, Millennials desire to be treated as an equal to their bosses and managers in the workplace. However, even though Millennials appear very comfortable in their middle-class lives, they are the most medicated generation ever bred. According to reporter Julie Grant (2004), "Dr. Michael Hogan was chairman of President Bush's Commission on Mental Health in 2002. He says one in five kids has some mental health disorder, such as anxiety. One in ten has serious enough psychological problems that it affects their schoolwork and home life." Furthermore, today's teens and young adults are more obese and unhealthy than any previous generation. New trends in self-mutilation such as "cutting" have evolved, and many members of this generation seek escapism through violence in video games, music, television, and movies.

What has caused this dynamic shift from a utopian world to the lives of the most depressed? Something has created an identity predicament. Is it our biology that is changing? Or is the modern world simply too difficult? Furthermore, what will this shift do to our future corporate and service related industries?

Parenting Styles of the Millennial Generation

There seem to be two views regarding the childhood of the Millennial. One view stems from the 'conditional love' philosophy, and the other from the aspect of 'unconditional love.' Generally, the Millennial childhood looks something like this: The parents of the Millennial generation are primarily Baby Boomers or older Gen Xers. Their primary ideal in raising their children was to offer protection, encouragement, empowerment, and security. According to *Making it Count! Educators*, Millennial parents wanted their children to feel as though they were special. They accomplished this through constant praise of high achievement, sheltered lives, high pressure for competition, rigid scheduling, and technology. According to Mark Urycki (2004), Millennials consider their parents some of the 'coolest' people they know:

> To get a handle on the Millennial Generation, take a look at their parents -- the Baby Boomers. They were raised on the civil rights revolution, anti-war protests, the women's revolution, and the invasion

of foreign competition. The Boomers were at war with their parents, helping to coin the phrase "generation gap." But who are the heroes of the millennial generation? The same answer keeps coming back: […]'Yeah, my parents. Parents, 'cause they've always backed me up. They've always been there, and they've always cared about my school.' If you can attach broad categories to a generation - and we are - the Baby Boomers revolted against the establishment to make a better world, the Gen X-ers reacted with a cynical, snarky attitude, and now the Millennials are coming along with an upbeat, confident outlook at taking over the world. And they'll probably do that faster than you think.

Millennials are generally most happy at home. They feel that their parents are supportive and loving, and sometimes even see their families as their friends.

    The parents of Millennials want the best for their children, and push until they receive the results they deem worthy. Some parents punish mistakes and failures by denying words of encouragement or endearment. However, when a child succeeds compliments shower him/her and the parents share in their child's successes. This is how successful adults are bred.

However, there are other sides to this generational childhood that are not as glamorous. Critics of 'conditional love' claim that the constant pressure to "be the best" is doing lifelong damage. According to Jim Taylor PhD (n/d):

> One of the dangers to a child's success and happiness occurs when parents use their love as a weapon to threaten and control their child. Love becomes a weapon when parents make their love conditional on their child's success or failure. Says the novelist John Steinbeck, "The greater tumor a child can have is that he is not loved, and rejection is the hell he fears." This type of conditional love is called outcome love, and it can be communicated openly or subtly to children. Some parents become so invested in their child's achievements that they actively reward success and punish failure. These parents lavish their children with love when they succeed and withhold love when they fail. They reward success by giving their love freely and expressively in the form of effusive praise and physical contact such as hugs and kisses. They also give outcome love materially by buying sometimes extravagant gifts when their children succeed.

The Baby Boomers want the most for their family, and they hold firm to the belief that their "babies" can do anything. Children have become the next step of 'keeping up with the Joneses." All of this due to the capitalistic idealism bred in the parents of the Millennials. Children have become a commodity for parents social statuses, even when the credit cards are declined, if their child is the best in the school district, they have succeeded as individuals.

Therefore to the unknowing witness, the childhood of the young Millennial seems 'picture perfect.' Increasing debt and mortgage payments afforded a life of luxury to these children; however, they have never known a truly humanistic life. They have been naively exposed to capitalism of the developed world, and they are treated more like the new widescreen-television or dog doing tricks than an equal and valuable member of the society at large.

Teaching Styles and Requirements of the Millennial Generation

Millennials have had a very different model of education than any previous generation. With the Baby Boomers, school was most likely an extension of home. Students were taught what they needed to know to get quality jobs with large companies. Authority figures in the school were to be feared and respected. When mistakes were made or rules were broken, the baby boomer would likely find himself swatted or having a chat with the principal. Parents believed in the school authority, and trusted the other authority figures over their children. GenX was raised much the same way. With the busyness of young Baby Boomer parents, GenX was often neglected and home, and MTV became a major source of information about life, style, and 'fitting-in.' School was a boring place, just something to get through so that they could find jobs in the rising service industry. The Millennials, on the other hand, have been given very little freedom of opinion when it comes to education. Yuppie parents expect that their children will be the star football-player, cheerleader, valedictorian, or student-body president. Standardized testing has further set the competitiveness between the students in motion. Failure is simply not an option. In the schools, students *require* superior grades and test scores. Students confront teachers claiming not that they deserve a certain grade, but rather that they "need" an A.

Educators frequently complain when dealing with the Millennial generation. These students expect good grades, regardless of the work performed, and when they don't receive them teachers will get phone calls from the parents complaining about the grades given. Furthermore, students complain about boredom in the classroom, or are *defiant enough* to use their cell phones and iPods against school policy.

The Millennial generation expects schools to personalize education for their needs. They also assume that schools should keep up with technological trends. When these expectations are not met, the Millennial loses respect for the classroom and rarely continues to work at their full potential. Educators often feel like glorified babysitters (Textor, 2008). Students expect their teachers to coach, cater to their needs, and become friends with them. Educators are no longer allowed to criticize openly. Every criticism is taken heavily, and students of this generation who are criticized too often usually become reclusive or unresponsive.

Parents are becoming more and more intolerant of school authority and discipline procedures. Even as the Millennials are reaching adult-hood the soccer moms and hockey dads are still a vital part of their children's lives. According to "Teaching the Millennial Generation" (2006):

> Even in college, the apron strings are still staying tied fairly tight. In the Wall Street Journal on March 3, writer Sam Schulman noted that one college survey has reported that parents of college freshmen were in contact with their children as often as 15 times a day – and that more than one university 'has been forced to station security guards outside freshman

orientation sessions to keep anxious parents out.'

As shown, the primary problem with the Millennial generation is that they are rarely satisfied and will complain to their educators, their friends, and even their parents. They want new technologies, new information, and fast-paced learning, offered by extremely friendly educators. Their learning styles are much like the technology they use so often. They want a change every three months, when the newest and latest computer is offered on the market. However, educators realize that budgets and schools simply cannot afford us such luxuries. Schools do not have the capabilities to purchase new computers three times a year, nor do teachers have the time to stay ahead in their own training of the technologies being offered (see "Creating the Digital Classroom" for tools to bypass extreme costs of media literacy).
According to Neil Postman (1992), children seem to be stuck in the middle of media warfare. He explains that although schools try to teach and cater to students, oftentimes it is their personal television viewing and computer usage that complicates any educational program offered through lectures and books:

> Children come to school having been deeply conditioned by the biases of television, there, they encounter the world of the

printed word. A sort of psychic battle takes place, and there are many casualties—children who can't learn to read or won't, children who cannot organize their thought into logical structure even in a Simple paragraph, children who cannot attend to lectures or oral explanations for more than a few minutes at a time. They are failures, but not because they are stupid. They are failures because there is a media war going on, and they are on the wrong side at least for the moment. Who knows what schools will be like twenty-five years from now? Or fifty? In time, the type of student who is currently a failure may be considered a success. The type who is now successful may be regarded as a handicapped learner—slow to respond, far too detached, lacking in emotion, inadequate in creating mental pictures of reality (p. 16-17).

Postman's ideas of Technopoly, a society based solely on the positive ideas of technology, and technophiles, those who nearly worship the idea of technological innovation, have become self-evident in the developed world. He only saw these ideas taking place in the America nearly twenty years ago, however technology has been on the rise around the world, with very little resistance. It seems clear to me why children would anticipate and be dependent on new technologies. Their world has bred nothing less.

Zero-Tolerance discipline is another new phenomenon the Millennials are facing. Each student is held under the rigid accountability of school discipline, with the police force on stand-by for any misbehaviors. The ultimate authority over children used to be in the home and school; now children are accountable for their actions to law-enforcement agencies. There is no age of accountability, everyone is suspect; what was once considered childish behavior or play, is now against the law. According to Lawrence Grossberg (2005):

> Consider the following examples of the new zero-tolerance practices in public schools in the United States [...]:
>
> - An elementary school boy in Wilmington, North Carolina, was jailed for three days for writing a screensaver on school computers that said, 'The end is near.' [...]
>
> - An elementary school student in Chicago was arrested for splashing other kids by stomping in a mud puddle [...]
>
> - In March 2002, in Kansas

City, Missouri, third-graders were subjected to strip searches [...]

- In Florida, an eighteen-year-old National Merit Scholar was arrested and banned from graduation when police spotted a kitchen knife she had used to open boxes in her car.

Children are pleading for educators to not only *hear* them, but also to really *listen*. They have things to say and to explain, if only someone would give them the opportunity.

 A few options for classroom teacher and workforce manager have been presented to keep Millennials interested and understanding of their environment (Sheahan, 2006). First, educators should seek to keep them involved. Communicate with them as equals, not inmates; allow them to create ideas based on your lesson plans, and allow them to use multi-media resources to accomplish a task, creating a multi-media collaboration can be a lot more exciting for you and them than having them write a research paper (see Appendix A: Multi-Media Projects and Ideas for Creativity)

There are core differences between Gen X and the Millennials. With their consistent demands and need for attention, they appear deprived of a precious something in which the other generations sought comfort and security. That precious "something" or "somethings" has a lot to do with our society, the rise of capitalism, the digital age, and our fears of the modern world.

Millennials and the Digital Age

"They're known as Millennials — young adults whose gadgets are like appendages to them. They can't imagine life without their cell phones, iPods, computers and being online. As the Pew Internet & American Life Project astutely observed, they are 'digital natives in a land of digital immigrants' " (Chansanchai, 2006). As children, the Millennial generation watched the death of the cassette tape and rise of the CD, the phase-out of VHS and the phase-in of DVDs and now Blu-Ray and Hi-Def. Technology is a vital part of everyday life to the digital natives, and they are adamant that they have the latest gadgets, technological trends, and time-saving innovations.

With the vested interest in new and up-coming technologies, these youths are not a stranger to the idea of disposable technology. Many have thrown out hundreds, if not thousands, of dollars of old computer equipment, cassettes, CDs, and cell phones. Parents stand in awe as their children walk out of the store with a brand new computer and are already complaining about wanting the newer model that will hit the stores the next week.

A blogger from families.com explains some of the problems facing identities and social conditions in our new idea of disposable society:

> Are we susceptible to the disposable society syndrome? Last week we went to look at the price of a new printer. The printer we were looking at was $99AU. The printer cartridge to go in it was $219AU! 'That's ludicrous,' I said. 'It'd be cheaper just to keep buying a new printer.' Mick agreed, it's a crazy system. It made me think we have become a disposable society. Sadly that attitude carries over into our marriages as well. It sometimes seems when couples strike a rough patch and things aren't going well or the gloss has gone off the marriage, the easy option is to start thinking about divorce rather than thinking about how to work at and improve their marriage (Harcombe, 2009).

Are our youths affected by our, and now their, disposable attitudes? Can healthy, lasting relationships be made through friends, romantic partners, or families?

I argue that this could be one of the multiple missing links for the newest generation. This generation has very little security. Their idea of technology is a mirage over their existences. Furthermore, with the idea of 'conditional love,' which, as mentioned above, has become a very popular model of parenting-- nothing is stable. No relationship is strong enough to endure all, no appliance should be kept forever, and no student can be assured a place in the university or job market. The option of "try, try again" failure has become obsolete, not only in our technology, but also in our children.

Youth and the McDonaldization of Modern Society

Many scholars have commented on the extreme change of society since the 1970s. Whether it's Zygmunt Bauman (2000) and his idea of Liquid Modernity or George Ritzer's (2007) idea of the "something-nothing continuum" and our McDonaldization of everything, we can easily recognize that modern corporations have been changing our opinions of products, services, and business in general. Globalization and capitalism have changed the way the world does business. Service industries are at their peak, and machines and technology have replaced most labor-jobs. Laissez-faire capitalism dictates our economy and jobs are now rarely secure due to corporate cuts, sell-outs, bailouts, and re-distribution of assets.

Richard Sennett (1998) tells a story about a man named Enrico who worked a blue-collar job his entire life, made enough money to buy a home in the suburbs for his family, and lived comfortably by working hard and staying loyal to his job. Enrico's son Rico, has also done well for his family, and is the stereotypical idea of the modern upper middle-class. However, Rico's work ethic and environments are far different from his father's. Rico has changed jobs, locations, and friendships many times in his life, and his children are not stable in any place.

> Rico worries that his children will drift ethically and emotionally [...] Change's confusions and anxieties have bred in him this swing to the opposite extreme; perhaps this is why he cannot hold up his own life as an illustrative tale to his children, perhaps why, in listening to him, one has no sense of his character unfolding, or his ideal evolving.

Richard Sennett calls this modern-age of capitalism *The Corrosion of Character*. With the constant changes and new ideas of knowledge, are we losing our sense of self?

Peters and Besley (2006) also question the idea of globalization, McDonald-ization, and personal identities through looking at George Ritzer:

Ritzer also briefly considers a number of other theoretical perspectives for viewing McDonaldization, including postindustrialism, post-Fordism, and postmodernism, all of which share the assumption that somehow we have passed beyond the modern. He concludes that McDonaldization fits Fredric Jamesons's (1981) five characteristics of postmodern societies—association with late capitalism, superficiality, waning of emotion or affect, loss of historicity, and reproductive technologies—but he does not think that we face a mode of production that is fundamentally different. He does acknowledge, however, that McDonald's, along with malls and Disney World, is an example of 'new means of consumption.' Developments in the postwar era have revolutionized the ways we consume by rationalizing the structures of consumption. Clearly this has effects on the self.

Without, as Ritzer puts it, "something" places, places of community, lingering, physical relationships, or being recognized, is there a way to build a healthy sense of self? In a world of anonymity and coldness, identities and can easily shift daily, and no one would know the difference. Are our identities wholly our own or are they built on how others perceive them?

These are all questions that the Millennial generation faces daily. They may be five or six different Avatar identities on social networking sites or games; they may change their appearance and attitudes consistently. When they walk into a store or restaurant, no one knows them from one day to the next, nor does anyone care to know them. Much like the digital age, our capitalistic society has created a community of strangers, and very little security therein.

Millennials as "the Other"

Many observers can recognize that today's youths, especially in the working class, are seen as a top public enemy, probably only second to foreign terrorists (and most media-related images of terrorists stem from this age group). In the United States, this is partly caused by the competition between the parents. Not only are the children down the street not 'good enough,' but they may also be dangerous. Hostility from children has been on the rise according to media outlets and victims of in-school crime. What has created this difference, if indeed one exists, and what can we do as a society to aid in this crisis?

According to one of the top scholars of the prejudice over the youth, Lawrence Grossberg (2005), kids are silently viewed as the primary enemy to American society:

> As youth culture increasingly comes to be seen as 'the dark force that walks among us,' youth comes not only to represent everything that has gone wrong in this country but in the end to be the cause of it. Children come to be seen as intrinsically evil, as variations on the theme that John DiIulio of the Brookings Institution [...] described as the rising wave of superpredators—'juvenile sociopaths, radically impulsive, brutally remorseless.' Whenever youths commit a crime, the coverage points to a generational shift that is metaphysical: for example, consider the headline 'Heartbreaking Crime: Kids without a Conscience' (p. 18).

Grossberg (2005) continues to explain that most people see these changes as purely biological. Kids are changing, and it's without reason. They are alien beings in our land. He quotes an article by Brett Easton Ellis, a prominent figure of GenX:

> 'Teens are running roughshod over this country—murdering, raping, gambling away the nation's future—and we have the bills for counseling and prison to prove it. Sure not all kids are bad—but collectively, they're getting worse. Why should we blame ourselves?'

Why should the older generations blame themselves? According to Mary Kay Blakely, the author of *American Mom:*

> 'The fact that boomers are turning out to be as strict or stricter than their parents may be a matter of envy rather than fear.... We have never felt like grown-ups, and we are absolutely fighting age tooth and nail. My generation has no experience in moving over, it's always been the biggest.' (Grossberg, 2005).

Grossberg (2005) also cites Mike Males, "Adult anger at teenagers is proportional to our anger at getting old. It makes us furious that teens can do so many things so effortlessly, that they have such flat stomachs" (p. 84).

A. Ferguson (2000) has also done quite a bit of research regarding low-income youths, especially African American males. Her book, *Bad Boys*, discusses how public schools predestine the lives of many students. Teachers who consistently state that children are bound for prison or a life on the streets is very harmful to young students. She argues, however, that most educators do not see African American male students as children. "These are children who are not children. These are boys who are already men. So a discourse that positions masculinity as "naturally" naughty is reframed for African American boys around racialized representations of gendered subjects. They come to stand as if already adult, bearers of adult fates inscribed within a racial order" (p. 96). Furthermore, schools inflict punishments such as isolation rooms, security guarded detentions, or better yet, suspensions where other students can learn from their mistakes, and where they can be put even further at risk by ending up on the streets.

Henry Giroux (1996) also studies racial issues and the working class in American society. In his book *Fugitive Cultures: Race, Violence, and Youth* he points out that the media ignites white panic not only toward the working class African American society, but also against the youth as a whole. Today's youth have very little in which to seek comfort. They are inheriting a slumping economy, deteriorating natural world, and massive debt.

> Held hostage to the bankrupt reality of modernization, many youth find themselves facing an economic future in which there will be an excess of service jobs but few viable economic opportunities. Such opportunities will be needed to propel large numbers of youth, with the exception of the most privileged, into a future often associated with a middle-class dream of home ownership, a

comfortable lifestyle, and job security. The dreams of a better life that were on the horizon for earlier generations of youth appear dysfunctional within a declining economy that condemns a vast number of working-class white and black youth to minimum-wage, low-skill, part-time work. Youth between the ages of fifteen and twenty-nine not only have the highest unemployment rate in the labor market, but polls further indicate 'that 75% think they will be worse off than their parents.' (p. 12).

The youth have to adapt to the new-world order. They may seem distant and different than many of the other "older" generations, and that is probably true. However, other generations could share a similar dream for their lives, a dream that no longer exists.

Millennials as Trans-National and Active Citizens

Millennials have found traces of security and comfort through their peers and their like-experiences. This is the first generation that could be called multi or trans-national. According to Eric Greenberg and Karl Weber (2009) "Millennials believe they have more in common with young adults of their generation in other countries than they have with Americans of older generations." Through sharing stories and experiences with youths around the world via online chat rooms, instant messaging, gaming, and social networking sites, many of these youths believe that they can join with others around the globe and create a positive change in the world. According to one survey, Millennials agree that the rise of technology pulls them together more than any other event in their lifetimes (Greenberg, 2009).

When the youngest of the Millennials reaches voting age around 2016, they will easily control the voting block with 90 million young voters. They are increasingly liberal, and in 2008 constituted 22% of the democratic votes. Millennials, despite media claims and general ideas are, more often than not, interested in the world, politics, and news. According to *The New Politics Institute*:

> The Millennials are an unusual generation, not like young people we have seen for a long time. As first noted by generational analysts William Strauss and Neil Howe, they are not individualistic risk-takers like the Boomers or cynical and disengaged like Generation Xers. Signs indicate that Millennials are civic-minded, politically engaged, and hold values long associated with progressives, such as concern about economic inequalities, desire for a more

multilateral foreign policy, and a strong belief in government (Leyden, 2007).

Although some are cynical regarding the motives of politicians, partisans, and corporate loyalties, Millennials generally think that they can make positive changes for future generations in energy resources, the economy, and internationalization.

This generation prides itself on being idealistic and informed. However, what is being taught to these children in the classroom? They will be making crucial choices for our future. What will help them make good choices in our critical age? Should we depend on bubble-tests or real-life skills developed through problem-solving tasks, collaboration, and thinking independently?

Conclusion

Research shows that Millennials are not a perfect generation. They are facing an identity crash of their nation, their world, their communities, and themselves. With the rapid changes and shifts in their societies, they have to adapt quickly and sometimes these adaptations create problems within the self and their personal disciplines. The problems at hand are due to greediness of our capitalistic desires as a society, models of parenting, and our outdated school system. Educational policy shifts are one way we could make a positive change for the Millennials as well as future generations. Joel Spring (2007) argues that our education system was originally built to create workers in our growing work force. The ideas conveyed and lessons taught were so that students could leave the schoolhouse and find a job without companies having to spend on training. However, times have shifted, and even though our schools still teach the same curriculum, employees are having to be further trained in their fields, because the intensity of career paths has increased so much in the last century. With our increasing luxuries, our lifestyles may be easier, but studies show they are not happier. " 'This... tremendous rise in average purchasing power was reflected in almost all households having an indoor toilet, a washing machine, telephone, color television as well as a car; ... this tremendous rise in material well-being was accompanied by a modest *decrease* in average happi-ness' " (p. 7). "In the new paradigm, educational policy is focused on longevity and subjective well-being rather than economic success" (p. 2).

This chapter was intended to show that Millennials have not had a "picture-perfect" existence. In fact, they may be the most insecure, depressed, judged, and lonely generation

America has ever seen. Yet, they have shown that they are interested in making changes. Furthermore, they insist that changes have to start with the schools. We don't have time to continue with our out-dated methods of education, educational policy requires urgent attention, and the new paradigm of education needs to be instilled in teachers and parents around the world. Our children can no longer be considered merely achievement competitors or disciplined robots. They need to be loved and cared for as children. They, much like our society as a whole, should be given time to learn from their mistakes and allowed to gradually shift into steady and strong individuals.

SECTION II

The Problems Surrounding American Schools

Chapter 3

Fostering a Cosmopolitan Student In a World of Tests, Extreme Capitalism, and Cross-Cultural Comparisons

Jefferson told us where to look to see if a nation is a success. He did not say to look at test scores. Instead, he said to look at 'life, liberty, and the pursuit of happiness-

Yong Zhao

Modern transnational corporations and the spread of capitalistic ideas around the world have led to super-speed globalization. Teachers in various nations are pushed to build the brightest and best students in the race toward the next superpower. However, through our creation and use of standardized testing and cross-cultural comparisons, we are neglecting and losing our creative thinking and critical perceptions of what we learn. Teachers are teaching to "the test," and students are learning to test, without any real life skills. This is creating a generation of confused workers, disposable academics, and perhaps worse than all of this, unfulfilled individuals. Can we create a new paradigm of education from here? Furthermore, once created, would it ever be applied? Can a critically thinking, cross-cultural, cosmopolitan citizen be fostered in this environment? If so, how do the major thinkers in educational policy suggest we accomplish this?

Capitalism, Cross-Cultural Comparisons, and Standardization

Terry Herndon (1981) of the New York Times addressed the fears of Reaganomics in his article "Is Public Education a Casualty of Reaganomics?" He describes the changes like this, "As the price of Reaganomics becomes clear, Americans are becoming edgy. Teachers are downright nervous. We who are the true believers in public education are nearly frantic. In the big budget fight of 1980 we saw the President strive for a 30 percent reduction in Federal aid to education."

After the effects of Reaganomics hit the middle-class, everything in education and American capitalism shifted for the worse. The rich received a major tax cut from 70% of their earnings to 28% in seven years (Ending Reaganomics, 2009). Naturally this loss of government funding had to affect certain public programs and public spending, such as disability, welfare, and naturally, public education. The best education offered shifted in many locations from the public schools to the private sector due to expenses of teacher training and costs of facilities. Naturally, only the wealthy could afford to send their children to these private or charter schools.

Inner city schools saw massive cuts in their liberal arts programs, such as music, art, drama, and speech. And suburban schools found it increasingly difficult to offer extensive band programs, foreign language beyond the basics, and theatre. Increased standardized testing dictated that the liberal arts were unnecessary to students' education. The media portrayed standardized testing as a good rubric for parents to adequately judge the school district their children attended, the teachers therein, and the information their children were being taught. Furthermore, this testing allowed for better cross-cultural comparisons. The tests showed that American students were, and still are, consistently behind many Asian nations in math and science.

No Child Left Behind (NCLB) was enacted in 2002, after President Bush's proposal of the act in 2001. This legislation meant that federal spending to education would increase, but only to the schools with the best standardized test scores. The foundation of NCLB lies in the idea that students in every grade, regardless of state or district, should share the same knowledge.

There are many problems with NCLB and America's schools that are forced to participate in this program. The best schools, due to funding and label, are the schools that "teach to the test," the idea that teachers review the practice tests and teach students only the information which will be found on the test. Students from these schools are receiving very little, if any practical guidance of how to apply their knowledge outside of the classroom, or how to live as successful adults in the "real world."

The schools that fail to comply with NCLB are labeled as "Needing Improvement." District funding is cut dramatically, and oftentimes parents will move their children out of the area. There is an incentive against these schools, against lower-achieving students, and also against the highest-achieving students. Low achieving students cause the schools expectations to be set lower, and higher achieving students are not important to the regulation, and spending is not set for gifted or accelerated learning. The hope of NCLB is that every American student will have the same knowledge and same skill sets when they graduate from High School. Since there are very few individual characteristics that are built upon in the schools, it leaves students feeling as though they are just a number. The earliest stages of "the loss of the individual."

The Loss of the Individual

Through inadequate schooling, our suffering economy, and consistent job losses, the American citizen's sense of self is depleting. George Ritzer's (2007) idea of McDonaldization, the "something-nothing" continuum, and Zygmunt Bauman's (2000) Liquid Modernity can be seen throughout all cities and towns in the developed world. No longer are members of a community recognized and known by neighbors and friends in the local stores and restaurants (the idea of "something"). McDonalds and Wal-Mart have taken over ("nothing"). Through this sterile society, people are able to change their personal identities nearly daily, and very few would recognize the difference. McDonald's workers don't know you, nor do they care to get to know you. You are just a number, and your personal identity does not matter.

Ideas of ethics, moral behavior, and loyalty shift consistently (Liquid Modernity). The speed of technology has left us as a disposable society. We collectively throw away millions of dollars of "old" technology annually. Not only are our children being raised in an environment where "things" don't matter, but they are also seeing their relationships through the same light. If a marriage isn't working, get a new one. If a friendship is too difficult to deal with, don't bother. If a job is too hard, go down the street, you'll find another career path.

Richard Sennett (1998) introduces many stories with the same outcome in his book *The Corrosion of Character.* He tells a story of an immigrant, Enrico, and his steady career, happy family, and home in the suburbs. Later he mentions Enrico's son, Rico, who, 25-years after his father's happy story, has moved consistently, and feels as though his identity as well as the identity of his children can never take root in the shaky foundation of the American workplace. He also reveals a New York bar-owner named Rose, who went to work in advertising only to find herself on a slippery slope of shallow people and the inability to get ahead. All of these changes, Sennett argues, have occurred in the past thirty-five years.

We can blame capitalism, government, and society for many of these fears, changes, and losses. However, in order to make a change, we have to start with our youth. We can begin to see a positive difference by instilling in out students a sense of personal strengths, cosmopolitan understanding, and a strong background in critical thinking, creativity, and problem solving.

Cosmopolitanism

To clarify my ideas of cosmopolitanism, I intend to look more into the works of Stuart Hall and Martha Nussbaum than the works of Kant. I believe that Cosmopolitanism is a work of the self, choice, capabilities, and action, not of natural governance or fate. Since Diogenes of Sinope around 400 B.C., the founding father of the Cynic movement, many have been aiming to live as a "citizen of the world." However, cosmopolitanism is generally second thought to nationalism, patriotism, and, of course, capital gain.

Martha Nussbaum has written, taught, and spoken extensively about Cosmopolitan theory and its relation to politics, society, and education. In Martha Nussbaum's 2008 essay and speech entitled "Education for profit, education for freedom," she shares that she is not unfamiliar with the failures of our modern policies and systems. She expresses that most countries are so eager to make profit and sustain their economic status, that trade and business are their sole priority. In this anxiety, education is quickly being lost to the game of profit. In the opening sections of this paper, she narrates four key mistakes that nations, especially centered on the U.S., have made regarding education. First, she examines the fall of 2006, when Margaret Spellings, the United State's Secretary of Education, released information that the U.S. was solely interested in expanding knowledge of the sciences and engineering for fast market gains. The report did not mention the arts, humanities, or critical thinking. Secondly, she mentions that the president of Harvard, Lawrence Summers, travelled to India in 2006 and hosted a three-day event called "Harvard in India." He presented that he eventually aims to dissolve subjects based in ethical reasoning and critical thinking, not only in the U.S., but also around the world. Thirdly, in 2005, Nussbaum reported being on a retreat where she spoke of teaching youths to think imaginatively and creatively. The presentation was geared to a set of teachers. She realized, sadly, that she was in a minority, as most of the teachers were more interested in thoughtless facts and wealthy family traditions. The last example she shared was a planned speech at a University's Liberal Education event. The event was cancelled, because the president of the University decided that such a liberal exhibition wouldn't make a "splash" (p. 2-3).

      Without a steady future in Liberal Education, democracy, and cosmopolitan thought, how can we adequately apply the capabilities approach to our lives, or attempt to evolve and create a global world? Educators and parents must realize the necessity for a firm foundation in lifelong learning and strong educational policies built around the arts, languages, humanities, and sciences. If we do not offer this well-rounded education to our youth, we will create a world of similar specialists and nothing unique. Furthermore, lifelong learning will diminish considerably, and the role of our technology will be not be used to its full potential.

Furthermore, relating to laissez-faire education reforms, and extreme capitalism Nussbaum (2008) expands:

> Given that economic growth is so eagerly sought by all nations, too few questions have been posed, in India as in the U. S., about the direction of education, and, with it, of democratic society. With the rush to profitability in the global market, values precious for the future of democracy, especially in an era of religious anxiety, are in danger of getting lost (p. 3).

Not only would we build a shallow foundation of competitors and not collaborators, we would also shake the groundwork of democracy, by creating a public who may not be able to think for themselves. They would only be capable of listening and responding to what they are told.

Nussbaum (2008) argues that education based in cosmopolitan thought is the only way we can counter these issues:

> We should have no objection to good scientific and technical education, and I do not suggest that nations should stop trying to improve in this regard. My concern is that other abilities, equally crucial, are at risk of getting lost in the competitive flurry, abilities crucial to the health of any democracy internally, and to the creation of a decent

world culture and a robust type of global citizenship, capable of constructively addressing the world's most pressing problems. These abilities are associated with the humanities and the arts: the ability to think critically; the ability to transcend local loyalties and to approach world problems as a "citizen of the world"; and, finally, the ability to imagine sympathetically the predicament of another person.

With these ideas, merged with her capabilities approach, a truly cosmopolitan education could begin to be offered.

Another leader of Cosmopolitan theory and education is Stuart Hall. Hall's primary argument is that Cosmopolitanism is often mistaken as being neo-colonialistic. This meaning that the United States pushes their ideas of Cosmopolitan living into the rest of the world. He argues that many times globalization is merely a way for capitalistic society to impose itself onto poorer nations:

> The decolonization that occurred at the end of World War II, often hailed as 'setting the colonial world free', was in fact marked by three broad stages redefining relations between the developed West and the rest. In the first phase, fundamental relations of neocolonial dependency were established between the developed and underdeveloped worlds in the context of the Cold War. ...the

Cold War was fought out largely by proxy on post-colonial terrain. In the second phase, 'structural adjustment' regimes were imposed by the West on the developing world, via international organizations coupled with massive indebtedness through the banking system. More recently, with the collapse of the Soviet empire and the rise of the US to single super-power hegemony, an unholy alliance of global corporate forces, collusive indigenous elites, and legal and illegal armies on the loose has been able to treat the world's poor and the societies of the South as open marketplaces, repositories of scarce resources, and reservoirs of cheap labour (pp. 27-28).

Hall (2006) in an interview with Pnina Werbner further states that he agrees with teaching children the ideas of cosmopolitanism. "The more we think about passing on the values of critical openness, you know, of respectful but not subservience to difference, of a democratic culture, questioning […] Why are they in positions of power? […] We ought to be teaching a cosmopolitan curriculum […] We are a mixed up multi-cultural society." He continues to suggest that students should be aware of people in power, their abilities, and how to live in a multi-cultural environment.

Overall, Stuart Hall and Martha Nussbaum urge governments, schools, and parents to realize and see their faults. The faults of wanting instant gratification, of teaching only trade--not liberal thinking, and of keeping the population at large quite uninformed. Teachers should include critical assessments and liberal thinking in their curriculum and push students to rationalize information and think about it seriously, striving to come up with personal thoughts and ideas, not mere rote learning.

Creative and Critical Thinking

The Chinese-American scholar, Yong Zhao, has offered a lot of insight regarding the differences and similarities between school and students in China and in the United States. Zhao (2008) shows that American workers are far more expensive than their Chinese and Indian colleagues:

> In part, the commission's report says: "Today, Indian engineers make $7,500 a year against $45,000 for an American engineer with the same qualifications. If we succeed in matching the very high levels of mastery of mathematics and science of these Indian engineers — an enormous challenge for this country — why would the world's employers pay us more than they have to pay the Indians to do their work? They would be willing to do that only if we could offer something the Chinese and Indians and others cannot.

Zhao (2008) continues to explain that throughout

their short history, Americans have been known for their creativity, problem solving, and critical thinking. Their original system of education was based on happiness and leading a fulfilled life. "Jefferson told us where to look to see if a nation is a success. He did not say to look at test scores. Instead, he said to look at 'life, liberty, and the pursuit of happiness' " (Zhao, 2009). However, recently the United States has been far more interested in cross-cultural comparisons of test scores, competitive markets in math and science, and the No Child Left Behind act. Zhao (2008) looks to Daniel Pink with regard to his idea of the ideal educational model for American students. "The right brain-directed (R-directed) skills (simultaneous, metaphorical, aesthetic, contextual and synthetic) are the new ones Americans should acquire because jobs that use the left brain-directed skills (sequential, literal, functional, textual and analytic) are being outsourced to Asia and machines."

The Indians and Chinese have been creating new models of education that are based on cultivating right-brain aptitudes. The United States has been creating just the opposite. No Child Left Behind has created a student population and a group of educators only interested in the sequential, functional, rational talents of Mathematics, Vocabulary, and Science reasoning through right and wrong answers.

Zhao (2008) concludes by saying that in order to remain competitive in the global market,

American education has to aim at not killing creativity. We must allow our students to be individuals with individual talents that teachers in the classroom can recognize and praise. He states that there is no practical way to "teach" creativity, but plenty of ways to kill it. Teachers, governments, and parents are the only tools we are given to cultivate the critical thinking, creativity, and problem solving skills that our students are known to possess:

> Instead of becoming more like others who are eager to be more like Americans, American education needs to be more American — to preserve flexibility, protect individuality and promote multiple intelligences. American education also needs to become more global — adopt a global perspective, add foreign languages and cultures and advocate global citizenship.

Conclusion: The Necessary New Paradigm of Education

As mentioned throughout this chapter, reforms at this juncture should not be optional, but mandatory. Specialized talents per individual are not recognized in our current system, and increased standardization deflates most children's sense of self, their idea of personal identity and growth, as well as their ability to see their natural talents besides Math, Reading, Science, and American History.

Joel Spring (2007) argues that students should be given the opportunities in school to grow into individuals who focus on "longevity and subjective well-being rather than economic success" (p. 2). He points out that through our rise in technological conveniences, we have seen a steady decline in overall happiness. Furthermore, Spring (2007) states that schools should be held accountable, and that individual successes should be fostered and talent, including creativity, should never be lost.

We can only manifest these changes through a grassroots movement. Even though testing and standardization is still a part of every teacher's experience, we have to recognize individual, as well as collective, talents and build upon them. When students recognize their potential outside of testing and regulations, they can begin to develop into fulfilled individuals and member of society. "In the new paradigm, students actively participate in increasing their capabilities and fostering conditions for a long life and happiness" (Spring, 2007).

Chapter 4

Pitfalls to Standardized Testing: Falling Behind in the World of 21st Century Skills

Increased test scores on a high stakes test do not necessarily translate into increased learning for students-

Karen Langenfeld

In the last sixty years, education policy has become a national issue. In 1958, as a response to Russia's launch of Sputnik, Congress passed the National Defense Education Act. This act funded specific technological programs including mathematics and science. In the early 1980s, education became focus after the release of <u>A Nation at Risk</u> report. This report provided alarming data on how our students were doing while in school, but also looked at adults the amount of adults that were illiterate. The issues noted in this report are still issues plaguing are education system today. America educational policy changed dramatically eighteen years later, when President George W. Bush signed the No Child Left Behind Act into law in 2001. The principle behind NCLB is great, who would want their child left behind. Unfortunately, the failure in the administration and development of the law has not improved student achievement like it was designed to do. Instead, the law is restricting teachers and the curriculum, which eventually hurts students when it comes to being ready in a globally "charged" world. Schools have become "factories" of producing students who can fill in "bubble" tests. Teachers are so busy "teaching to the test" because they fear losing their jobs. This method of teaching focuses on the test, but fails to address the 21st Century skills of creativity, collaboration, critical thinking, and communication. Should other measurements be in place to measure student achievement instead of one "high stakes" test? Is the United States behind in mathematics and science when compared with other industrialized countries? Are the standards between countries comparable or is it looking at two different things? The NCLB mentality, high stakes tests, and the failure to teach 21st Century skills are not preparing our students for the future of global competition for jobs.

To understand how our students are losing the opportunities to develop critical thinking and creativity skills, we must understand some issues surrounding the No Child Left Behind Law. No Child Left Behind is a great concept, but a nightmare to administer. The law is based on four principles or "pillars". The pillars focus on accountability, more freedom for districts, more choices for parents, and proven educational methods ("Four Pillars"). Some issues that will be explored include the goals of the law as well as the penalties. The issue of funding and teacher/school accountability will also be discussed.

The goals are set high and unrealistically. "The number of students that pass state reading and math tests must increase every year until 100 percent of students are passing by 2013-2014 school year" (Peterson, 2005). In the case of special education students, it is absurd to think that high school students reading at the 3rd Grade level will be at the high school grade level. This is a great goal, but probably unattainable. In some cases, these students who often have various "accommodations" with test taking and homework have to take the test with no accommodations or services. Even with accommodations, the students struggle because the questions are above their knowledge base. In some districts, these students are sometimes put into their own subgroup which ultimately decides whether a district makes Adequate Yearly Progress (AYP).

"Schools and districts will be considered "in need of improvement," or failing AYP, if test scores in any group fail to meet state goals for two or more years" (Peterson, 2005). The mentality of penalizing instead of mentoring or rehabilitating sends the wrong message. This puts administrators and teachers in "defense" mode. Instead of penalizing, it would be beneficial to offer training and steps to get on track. In some cases, community training would be a great thing. The schools that suffer the most are the smaller schools and schools with lower socioeconomic status which usually means higher rates of diverse students. According to Au, 2005, small schools are most volatile. "All other arguments about testing aside, small schools are extremely "volatile" when it comes to measuring their progress statistically through standardized test scores. To be volatile in a statistical sense means that you may be subject to wild swings in test scores from year-to-year, grade-to-grade, and school-to-school" (Au, 2005). One main goal of NCLB is to reduce the achievement gap between low and high socioeconomic status and diversity differences. According to a 2005 report from the Northwest Evaluation Association, "The addition of high-stakes testing has not been shown to reduce the achievement gaps among students of different ethnicity. The AYP model currently in use in NCLB may not identify schools that are doing a good job of helping low performing students grow and could mask achievement gaps" (Cronin, 2005). This report released only years after schools were to be NCLB compliant, is probably still accurate today. Standardized testing cannot be the only measurement of our students. Schools should not be punished for not making AYP, but mediated in a positive way. The current process of putting schools on "watch lists" puts administers and teachers in defense mode. This process could also pull teachers from a struggling district to a district making progress, which leads to good teachers leaving tough schools. It is also challenging for rural schools to get highly qualified teachers to stay in their districts. "Many rural districts have had difficulty recruiting and retaining highly qualified teachers. Low salaries, remote locations, challenging student and school conditions make some rural locations less attractive to new teachers" (Jimerson, 2003).

Teacher and School accountability is very important and poor teachers and schools need assistance. One provision of NCLB is that all teachers should be "highly qualified". "Highly qualified" does not mean highly effective. "This law has nothing to do with improving learning. At best, it's about raising scores on multiple-choice exams. This law is not about discovering which schools need help; we already know. This law is not about narrowing the achievement gap; its main effect has been to sentence poor children to an endless regimen of test-preparation drills. Thus, even if the scores do rise, it's at the expense of a quality education" (Kohn, 2009).

Funding is low or non-existent. "The study argues there is unequal funding between schools in the city and the suburban areas. In addition, the study makes the case that there is a clear pattern of the under-funded schools becoming increasingly populated with students of color" (Renner, 2007). Regardless of socioeconomic status and race of students, the fact is our schools are not funded properly or there is a misuse of the money allotted. The current way of funding schools (through property taxes) is unfair to students who deserve to get fair and equal education. According to the report Illinois Kids Count 2009, "local revenues per pupil ranged from less than $2,000 in Posen-Robbins (southern Cook County) to more than $18,000 in Kenilworth (northern Cook)". This disparity cannot be made up even with the help of the state. When adding NCLB and Response to Intervention to the budget, funds are even more scarce to prepare and comply with these mandates. Most of the expense of NCLB will be absorbed at state level. This expense is often then passed to the district level because state funds are not released adequately. "Federal funding to compensate states and school districts for the mandates imposed by NCLB has been woefully inadequate so far" (Jimerson, 2003). According to Howard Gardner, PhD, "Since the mandates for equipping teachers to prepare students for the tests are underfunded, the whole impetus for the legislation is being undermined" (Kersting, 2003). Where some schools are thriving and investing in technology, others are struggling to pay basic expenses, which leaves some districts behind.

    The use of high-stakes testing as a way of accountability is unfair. High stakes testing provides a national benchmark on a test and is a comparing point when comparing students on a test. There must be other viable measurement tools instead of a standardized test. Another possible benefit is learning through the data produced from the test where the curriculum of the school is lacking. Studies have also found that "an increased sense of clear mission is the one positive attitudinal change to be documented from high stakes testing" (Langenfeld, 1997). Other than those two benefits, I believe that high stakes testing is detrimental to the curriculum and schools in general. One thing I'm experiencing within the classroom is a push for taking a day a week in order to prepare students for the test. "'Teaching to the test' means a concentration on skills that increase test scores regardless of the amount of knowledge the student actually possesses" (Langenfeld, 1997). Schools are also teaching test taking tips and recommending a good nights sleep and in some cases feed the students breakfast before taking the exam. One issue I have with high stakes and standardized testing is that a child in rural Illinois is being compared to a child in inner-city Chicago. These children may be the same age and in the same class, but their way and style of living is totally different. The test should take those issues into account and currently high stakes testing does not do that. Several studies have been conducted and have shown that test scores rose, but actual learning has not. The studies were done in the 1980s and 1990s, but can be applicable in this decade. According to Langenfeld, (1997), "increased test scores on a high stakes test do not necessarily translate into increased learning for students. The problems go beyond simple inflation of test scores, which is a serious concern from a measurement standpoint. These studies point to a frightening, but very real possibility that children will be systematically and deliberately labeled, excluded, and pushed out of the system altogether in order to improve test scores".

There have also been studies conducted that focus on the effect of high stakes testing on our students. "A number of psychologists, including Howard Gardner, PhD, warn that the testing legislation, however well-intentioned, will ultimately do more harm than good" (Kersting, 2003). In early grades, the length, the complexity, can impact a child's self-esteem. In addition to test anxiety and "failure mentality", "teachers believe tests cause stress, frustration, burn-out, fatigue, physical illness, misbehavior and fighting, and psychological distress" (Langenfeld, 1997). Another argument that currently has no correlation to high stakes testing but is being researched is the increased drop out rate of students. The studies that have been conducted have had mixed results. For example, Florida allows a student to take a competency exam up to five times beginning in 10th grade. This test is required to graduate high school. "The authors found that dropout rates increased only for students who were doing well academically and subsequently failed the tests. Dropout rates did not increase for students who already had poor academic records, or for minority students" (Langenfeld, 1997). The results are interesting. The students who are normally seen as drop outs continue, where those that are typically "good" students would have trouble passing and then become at-risk. Again, accountability is good thing, but I believe high stakes testing is hurting our students. One thing the high stakes testing studies do not have data on is the emotional and academic factors of students.

Teacher's feel that high stakes testing hurts students and increases teacher's stress levels and workloads. "Testing causes stress and frustration for both teachers and, reportedly, for students as well. Teachers reported decreased autonomy and ability to rely on their professional judgment" (Langenfeld, 1997). With implementation of RTI (Response to Intervention), school districts in Illinois are scrambling to be compliant by January 2010 with little state guidance and very few funds to work with. Many teachers across America believe the concept behind NCLB is good, but the administration and goals unrealistic. Having goals and holding schools is a step in the right direction, but penalizing districts is sending the wrong message to students and teachers as long as some improvement measures are being taken. It is important to note that teachers do want accountability. However, I and most other teachers believe that it shouldn't be based on one exam. Other assessments, for example, portfolios or project based assignments should also be included in "equation" for judging whether a school's students are learning. In his work <u>Classism and Education: NCLB, Regulated Knowledge, and Resistance (2007)</u>, Adam Renner states:

> "However, suggesting that one assessment—arbitrarily implemented at a particular point of a child's education and used to compare one year's students against the previous year's students—can measure a student's/school's/teacher's ability is simply proposterous. No sensible educator seeks to erase accountability in the system. Instead, what critical educators seek is a system of curriculum and assessment that is contextual, authentic, and rigorous, and contains wider goals and standards toward which success

is measured by growth, not an arbitrary cut-off score"

By limiting our students with standardized tests, we are not getting a clear picture of our student's strengths and weaknesses, therefore the tests are an inaccurate measurement of our schools.

This idea of high stakes testing and unrealistic goals set forth by NCLB is giving our nation the wrong mentality to succeed in the global market. We need to shift our schools from the idea of test preparation to preparing our students for real-life situations. Instead of spending endless hours practicing tests, we should be focusing on developing four needed skills our students will need regardless of what job you do. The four skills are communication, critical thinking, creativity, and collaboration. Each skill is important to being competitive in the workplace and in the global marketplace. We are no longer preparing our students for a local job, but we are preparing them for a "global" job. As educators, we spend a significant amount of time on test preparation. It is important to note how this preparation is affecting our students critical thinking skills. According to Boutelle (2009), "many educators and researchers worry that students and teachers are leaving behind not only a crucial component of a good education but also the skills necessary to lead a productive adult life: knowing how to assess, question and reason in order to make informed decisions, solve problems and communicate effectively".

As educators, one question we have is: how are we comparing to the rest of the world from an education standpoint? The National Center for Education Statistics (NCES) through a congressional mandate studies how the United States compares to other countries in the areas of Reading, Mathematics, and Science. NCES looks at three tests to compare the United States with other countries. The tests are the Progress in International Reading Literacy Study (PIRLS), the Program for International Student Assessment (PISA), and the Trends in International Mathematics and Science Study (TIMSS). Each test focuses on elements of Reading, Science, and Mathematics. Before we discuss these tests, it is important to note not all students from the countries participating take this exam. How is it possible for us to determine "how we are doing" if only a small sample of our nation's students are taking the exam? Do we know how many students and what "caliber" of students are taking the exams from other countries? Every three years the PISA is given and the results tabulated. Are these tests administered the same way? Are the test booklets the same? I feel that accurate measurements cannot be based solely on a standardized test. The United States results on the PISA in 2006 could not be tabulated to an error, so technically we do not know where we stand on reading literacy, we are using the data from the 2003 test. "PISA 2006 reading literacy results are not reported for the United States because of an error introduced when the test booklets were printing. Thus the reading literacy results described here come from the PISA 2000 and 2003" (NCES, 2009). If the tests are not printed and not compiled for the exam, would they be a valid measurement? My main argument is that standardized testing is not an accurate measurement of a student. External factors should be considered when overall student scores are assessed. Students in inner-city America when compared to students in suburban America are often at a disadvantage. We feel it is unfair to assess each group with the same assessment. According to Cress (1974), "Test performance reflects the interaction between capacity and the particular conditions of previous training and current test demands. It may thus be concluded that the cognitive potential of members of one cultural milieu cannot be assessed accurately by the tests of another culture".

A student that is measured solely on a standardized test isn't tested for the 21st Century skills students must have regardless of the job they have. The standardized tests that are used to test students do not translate to the skills needed in the workforce today. Assessments that are being used looks at basic reading and mathematics, but very little with technology and other skills needed to be competitive in global market. In her report, <u>Measuring Skills for the 21st Century</u>, Elena Silva (2008) states:

"most students take tests that are primarily multiple-choice measures of lower-level skills in reading and math, such as the ability to recall or restate facts from reading passages and to handle arithmetic-based questions in math. These types of tests are useful for meeting the proficiency goals of the federal No Child Left Behind Act (NCLB) and state accountability systems. But leaders in business, government, and higher education are increasingly emphatic in saying that such tests don't do enough. The intellectual demands of 21st century work, today's leaders say, require assessments that measure more advanced skills, 21st century skills. Today, they say, college students, workers, and citizens must be able to solve multifaceted problems by thinking creatively and generating original ideas from multiple sources of information—and tests must measure students' capacity to do such work".

This mentality of testing basic skills and not looking at the skills needed in the workplace is backwards. We need to be asking our colleges and employers what skills are needed and then adapt our curriculum and tests to their needs. The main problem with changing the test is expense and setting criteria for such assessments as portfolios, exhibitions, and projects. Opponents of other forms of assessment also argue that measuring the 21st

Century skills is a difficult task. According to Silva (2008), "The cost, time demands, and difficulty in scoring tests of these less easily quantified skills have slowed the adoption of such tests, as have concerns among civil rights advocates that these tests would erode progress toward ensuring common standards of learning for all students". It is time for reform, regardless the cost. Many students are leaving our secondary schools without the skills needed to compete in the world today. We cannot afford students leaving our buildings with the lack of communication and problem solving skills. Unfortunately, in our times of economic crisis, anything with "cost" attached to it is frowned upon. As Americans, we need to question, *is education a priority or is falling behind ok?* In 2006, the Commission on the Skills of the American Workforce issued a report <u>Tough Choices or Tough Times</u>. This report suggests that basic skills are needed, but not sufficient for success in the world. "Students need a strong foundation of basic skills, the commission asserts, but that alone is no longer enough for economic and job security" (Silva, 2008). This report written by Silva, addresses key issues that educators, administrators, and politicians need to look at and need to take action on immediately.

As educational policy has changed and continues to change, it is crucial that educators focus on skill sets students need to be successful in the global market. NCLB and high stakes testing are hurting our students. Our schools have become factories for bubble test takers instead of world problem solvers. Teacher and school accountability are necessary, but neither should be penalized, but they should be assisted and brought back to the standards they need to meet. NCLB's unrealistic goals automatically put administrators and teachers on the defense. This also puts stress on our students, which makes learning even more challenging. High stakes testing should not be the only measurement for student growth and achievement. Other alternatives, for example: portfolios, projects, and exhibitions are not pursued due to cost and the fear of "biased" results. Our current situation is not good and thousands of students are graduating without the skills needed. The time for reform is now.

SECTION III

Using Technology In The Globalized Classroom

Chapter 5

Creating a Globalized Classroom

Electronically we can go anywhere we want. It helps to break of the monotony of the classroom.-

Ozzie Smith

Classrooms around the world are facing rapid changes in modern society. Cross-cultural and cross-national comparisons are creating a global-race, and the English speaking countries are, at this point, still the dominant nations. However, India and China have a growing population and their educational policies are shifting to produce students who can work longer hours, produce more, and think more critically about problem solving than students from the United States or Europe.

Should Euro-centric nations aim to compete with this global force? Especially considering that both China and India have more honors students independently than the U.S. has a total student population? There is a vicious cycle surrounding International Education in our modern age. Europe and the Americas have been known for their creativity and problem-solving capabilities for centuries. However, we consistently lag behind our Asian counterparts in mathematics and the sciences. Now, we are attempting to compete mathematically with Asia, and we are losing our focus of creative thinking. China, Japan, and India, contrastingly, realize that in our modern age we can depend on machines for our knowledge in mathematics and functional understanding- their students are focusing more and more on the liberal arts and humanities.

This chapter will focus on ideas regarding this global force and the competition therein. I argue that we, as educators and educational policy writers, should not continue our competition for dominance, but rather shape our students into global thinkers. Our classrooms shouldn't be modeled to produce factory-line workers, but rather fulfilled citizens of the world.

Problems

Schools have been focused on producing workers for many decades. The problem with this is that the workforce is changing, and our classrooms are not. Factory lines are based more around machinery and how to operate the machinery than ever before, and computers handle most of our monotonous labor.

Global competition has soared in recent years. Outsourcing has allowed companies to hire Indian and Chinese employees for a tenth of the cost of an American with the same skill sets. Trans-National Corporations pride themselves in cutting-costs wherever available, and company/employee loyalty has changed drastically for the worst. With these shifts, the American workers and employers are not only self-defeated, but are also involved in an involuntary ethical shift toward career-based apathy.

Workers are expected to have a common knowledge of modern technology and world affairs. Promotions are based on these skills. However, our schools are more interested in pumping students with the same knowledge we pumped in the 1950s: Reading, Writing, and Arithmetic.

Our students will be involved in careers that are not yet invented. In fact, in the past decade hundreds of new career opportunities have sprung out of our new technology. In the classroom, these students learn to memorize information that is readily available to the masses. Shouldn't we as educators be teaching them how to quickly and accurately find the information they need instead of forcing them to memorize outdated textbook materials?

A firm knowledge of technology is an obvious step that must be taken by all schools worldwide. We must also take steps daily to open the minds and eyes of our students to the globe. For centuries our biggest interest was the self and identity in the nation or community, now the self and identity are seen through a world vision.

Constructing a Global Classroom Ideologically

The most crucial part of a student's global understanding comes from their families and their teachers. Just as these mentors can kill or build upon creativity, so can they kill or build upon a student's global awareness. Educators must be willing to be lifelong learners of the world, and never be satisfied with prejudiced reasoning or nationalistic ideas without first examining all sides of the situation.

In the classroom, students should also be encouraged to think deeply about words, ideas and comments. When a student or teacher says, "we believe…" or "we think…", what does this really mean? Who is "we"? "We" as the world? "We" as a nation? "We" as young people? "We" as a classroom? "We" as a family, etc. There are very dangerous words. We/us, they/them, culture, identity, and so on. *We* as global educators should aim to offer our students guidance on how to approach these words and how to use them wisely.

Learning to think openly about the world and how to place oneself within the world is a task that most of us spend our lives trying to figure out. However, I believe that without national prejudices or seeking to find differences, it could be a lot easier.

After 9/11, it is impossible for us, as American citizens, to ignore globalization. That was the penultimate effect of clashing civilizations and national idealism. The rest of the world is here, and now, and we cannot avoid it.

The world is consistently surrounding all of us, whether it is on the television, through the computer, in the home through the production of possessions, or international travelers, students, or residents living in the community. We cannot pretend that the world is far away any longer.

Not only should we focus on passing ideas to our students, but we should also include the community in our efforts. Many people have fears surrounding the idea of globalization. These fears are due, generally, to a lack of knowledge about the subject. Involving parents, administration, and community leaders in our efforts at global educators creates a unity of knowledge that helps our schools, local businesses, and youth.

Constructing a Global Classroom Physically

A "global" classroom should introduce students to new ideas that they would not find in a standard nationalistic society. World maps can be found in most classrooms; however, even a traditional map creates a sub-conscious dominance of the U.S. and Europe over, or "on-top-of" Africa and South America. A reversed map is an excellent way for students to see and realize that there is no true top or bottom to our world, and that there are multiple ways one can view our globe.

Furthermore, classrooms in general are very small physical spaces. Save for books and games, there is no way for a child's mind to escape the space they are located. Incorporating a digital aspect to the classroom is an option for students to break free from the monotony of old-fashioned student life. Additionally, it literally places the "world" at their fingertips. See our chapters on "Creating the Digital Classroom" or "Tools for Students" for more information of how to accomplish this task. Also, the virtual, social network RezEd is a great community of educators interested in building a technologically advanced, global classroom.

Many teachers believe that pictures of people from around the world help to foster a more global student. However, I tend to question this reasoning. If we want to help students see themselves as "citizens of the world," should we show them their cultural differences before they have a chance to question or see their similarities? We all can easily see our differences. As teachers, we need to help them see their similarities. Instead of posting pictures on a bulletin board of "different places" and "different people," let them explore for themselves. Ask them to find photos of similarities between themselves and children around the world. After they explain how they are alike, post these photos around your classroom.

Our students must learn to coexist in a world of vast ideas and rapid change. And they cannot learn to do this without proper education.

Constructing a Global Classroom Project

Students have often been interested in having pen pals around the world. The funny part of this scenario is that the pen pals are generally speaking in a second-language. Pen pals from China and most European countries are learning English, and an American friend is an excellent way for them to practice their new skill. Our students are gaining an acquaintance and figuring out the functions of another country, but are not truly learning or practicing any specific skill sets. If your school offers foreign language training, having a pen pal write in English while your students write in the pen pal's native tongue is a much better and more involving way for students to "see" the world through a friend. However, this is not an option for most schools due to budgets and foreign language teachers.

Instead of having international pen pals, why not ask students to create multi-media projects without words that show what it is like where they live and have the international students do the same? This is an exciting use of video technology, computers, and music. They can then post their projects to a wiki or a ning, and it offers both sides a chance to practice and work on new skills needed for the 21st century along with fostering creative talents and offering a project geared around the liberal arts. Even schools with a tight budget can create this kind of involvement. Wikis and nings are free of charge. See our "Tools for Teachers" chapter on websites and opportunities to create multi-media projects for free.

A good resource for this activity is epals.com. ePals is a global site that connects learners and teachers around the world through a common interest in global affairs, the environment, politics, and history. Students communicate through blogs, digital storytelling, and forums. EPals matches schools based on language, interests, and age.

With technology all things are becoming possible. RezEd, a program offered by Global Kids, as mentioned earlier this chapter, previewed a new concept offered by many coastal universities to students of all ages in the Summer of 2009. The article announced the arrival of virtual study abroad. Students are now able to attend an international university in the nation of their choice from the comfort of their home or school. Not only are they able to attend classes online, but through a Second Life program, they are given Avatars and placed in a dorm, where they can comingle, go-out, and function in real-time with students from the host country. RezEd is free of charge, and easy to access. Prices of virtual study-abroad vary. It is a great extra-curricular activity, and may eventually gain enough universal acceptance and popularity to be used in the school.

Studies have shown that students spend on average 31 hours a week online ("Teenagers" 2009). If they spent half that time on a study-abroad program, how quickly could they learn about languages, people, and countries?

Imagine your students having a year-long project based on the experience of a virtual study-abroad program. The final essay or project about the experience would probably prove to be life-altering. Not only are students learning from these opportunities, but it is also expanding their curiosity about the rest of the world and giving them even further excitement about actually studying abroad at some point in their educational careers.

On a smaller scale, PBS offers a set of documentaries named *Wide Angle*, which promote stories from around the world that open discussion to real-life problems and global issues. The also offer free lesson plans to teachers and simple daily activities that can fit into a regular school day.

However we as educators choose to pursue starting a globalized classroom setting, it is sure to be a rewarding experience not only for the students, but also for us. It's important to remain imaginative and think of new ways to incorporate our vast and ever-closer globe to our students. Hopefully, a few of the ideas presented here will help spark your creativity and help you transform your classroom from School 1.9 to School 2.0.

Chapter 6

The Digital Classroom: Why and What it Looks Like

There are those who look at things the way they are, and ask why... I dream of things that never were, and ask why not?-

Robert Kennedy

The Importance of the Digital Technology

Anyone who has teenagers or works with teenagers knows that many hours are spent online or texting using mobile devices. Access to the personal computer and cellular phones is affordable and widespread. This report by PEW Internet and the American Life Project challenges me as an educator. It is vital that educators learn how to use the developing technology and teach our students the correct way and the benefits of using it. Often times, students use these new technologies, but when asked to use them for educational purposes, they act uninterested. For example, I started a Ning for forum discussions in my Speech class to discuss various issues. The students were very reluctant to get accounts and start discussions. However, in the first week of school I had friend requests from 10 of the 14 wanting me to be their friend on Facebook. Ning and Facebook are very similar, but students are reluctant.

The report specifically looks at Teens and Social Media. The study was conducted between October 23 and November 19, 2006. A sample of 935 teens between age 12-17 and parents were contacted by phone interview. The data in the report is now three years old. Some data is still accurate, but I believe mobile phones are more widely used then indicated in the report. The report is broken down into three sections: 1) Teens creating content 2) Communications and social media 3) Teens' online activities and gadgets.

The first section, "teens creating content," focuses on the idea that teens are leading the way in creating content. Teens are sharing videos, photos, creating social networks, and designing their own webpages. This section of the report looks at technology's accessibility to our teens. "Online teens have access to tools that can gain them widespread attention and notoriety—for better or for worse—in ways that simply were not possible under the traditional mass media model" (Lenhart, 2007). It is crucial, as parents and teachers, we intervene and make sure students know the dangers as well as the positives of creating content on the internet. "The data shows that the content creators are more likely to be girls between the ages of 15 and 17. Another interesting statistic shows that 52% of content creators live in suburban America versus urban or rural areas. The data also shows that those most likely to blog are from lower-income and single parent households. Could blogging be these teenager's voice and way to get the attention they are wanting? It is also interesting to note, the data shows that teens who are most active online also lead active lifestyles offline. "Those who are the most active online with social media applications like blogging and social networking also tend to be the most involved with offline activities like sports, music, or part-time employment" (Lenhart, 2007). Parents and teachers struggle to keep up with the new technology, but it is nearly impossible as technology sometimes evolves daily. This is true in the area of remixing content. 17% of online adults report remixing content when compared to 26% of online teens (Lenhart, 2007). We have to do a better job to "harness" the technology and direct our children on the correct and ethical usage of material.

The second section, "Communications and social media," focuses on the many ways teens communicate. Through the use of cell phones, instant messaging, texting, email, landlines, and face to face teens are using multiple ways to communicate with peers. As mobile technology has been made affordable and accessible, cell phones have become a major communication tool for teenagers. "Youth who own cell phones are considerably more likely to use their mobile phones to talk to friends daily than they are to pick any other option, with 55% of this group saying they use their cell phones everyday to talk to friends" (Lenhart, 2007). The data shows that content creators communicate more than those who do not create content. Text messaging is a "must" in most teenagers' lives. It is surprising this statistic was so low. According to the Teens and Social Media report, "61% of content creators text message compared with 40% of non-creators" (Lenhart, 2007). Teens that belong to a social network are also more likely to use text messaging as a way to communicate. The data shows that "67% of social network users have sent or received text messages, compared to just

38% of those not on social networks" (Lenhart, 2007). Teenagers have a very valuable tool that they carry with them everyday. Is there a way to "harness" this technology and make it a tool instead of a disruption?

The third section "Teens' online activities and gadgets" focuses on teenagers activity while they are online or gadgets they use to stay "connected" to their friends. The report found that 93% of teens use the internet, 89% use it from home (Lenhart, 2007). It is also interesting to note the number of teenagers and their access to various gadgets used to communicate. The data shows that 63% of teenagers own a cell phone, 51% own ipods, 72% own a desktop, and 25% own laptops (Lenhart, 2007). This data suggests that as adults we have to be "plugged in" to the world of technology and shows teenagers the proper ways to use these tools. A list of inexpensive technology ideas and tools is included in this chapter.

The data of the report "Teens and Social Media" by Pew Internet and American Life Project, challenges me as an educator of teenagers. The findings support my belief, opinion, and thesis that cellular phones and mobile devices are the wave of the future. As educators, we must find a way to embrace this technology instead of fight it. Ipods and cellular phones are wonderful tools that when used properly can be used for educational tools. As their identities develop, it is crucial for positive adult direction when using these technologies. Parents and teachers should be mindful on how they approach teens about their online profiles according to Danah Boyd from the University of California-Berkeley. Being strict might be a negative as well as being to lenient. "Teens often fabricate key identifying information like, name, age, and location to protect themselves. While parents groups often encourage deception to protect teens from strangers, many teens actually engage in this practice to protect themselves from the watchful eye of parents" (Boyd, 2007).

Boyd's writing "Why Youth (Heart) Social Network Sites: The Role of Networked Publics in Teenage Social Life" discusses why teens are engaged in social networking sites. She also discusses the term networked publics and how difficult it is to define the word "public". Boyd then focuses on four properties separating networked publics and unmediated publics. In her article, she looks at parental involvement, privacy issues, and the idea of teens fabricating their identities.

Designing the Digital Classroom

When designing the digital classroom an implementation plan needs to be made and followed. Planning and evaluation are two key elements when designing a digital classroom. The next few pages will focus on the implementation, funding, and evaluation. Towards the end of the chapter I will focus what elements, I include or would include within my classroom. Each element, will be discussed in the more detail in the "Tools for Students" and "Tools for Teachers" chapters. It is important to note that in the following paragraphs, the terms "technology program", is interchanged with "digital classroom".

Implementation and planning is probably the most crucial on whether a newly implemented technology program succeeds or fails. It is very important to set goals in order to achieve the most effective technology program. By doing early planning, a school can make changes to the program if a problem occurs. Another important reason for planning allows a school district to get the training the teachers need and allow them to purchase the best equipment to meet their goals. Before a school implements a technology program, it is a good idea to look at other schools technology programs and speak with the teachers and administrators about the pros and cons of their program. According to Steven Mills, "schools cannot expect to obtain gains in learner achievement from computer technology if it is not properly implemented (Mills, 1999). This not only applies to computer technology, but any type of technology, including cell phones and Ipods.

Another issue with implementation is funding. Right now, with our current economic state, schools are already operating on "tight" budgets. Grants exist but are very difficult to obtain. Many schools are only spending on "essential" items, in which technology is usually put off. An administrator with a good implementation plan will agree to replace a certain number of computers in a building every school year to reduce replacing an entire lab or school at once. In the case for other technologies, like interactive white boards, Ipods, etc. a good administrator will begin buying a certain number a year until the school is up on the most current technology it can afford. As I stated above, in a lot of cases, technology is not a priority and ultimately our students are left behind. It is important to note the knowledge our students gain with the technology is more important than the technology itself. Technology is the tool that the students are already adapting into their lifestyles. That is why it is important for us as educators to teach the correct way to use the technology.

     As a school or district revamps their technology and begins the process of creating the digital classroom, it is important to have teachers involved, for they decide how and when the digital equipment will be used within their curriculum. In order for a technology program to be successful in the classroom, the teacher must approve and accept the technological change and be willing to learn the new technology. If the teacher is not interested in learning, the program fails and then our kids fail. The study and research conducted by Dr. Steven C. Mills states that the main concern of teacher the early stages of technological innovation is management. His study looked at schools that were developing the

Integrated Learning System (ILS). According to Dr. Mills research, "The teachers in this study most often expressed awareness, informational, or personal concerns (Mills, 1999). Anytime new technology is implemented, there will be concerns. Feedback of any kind is good when implementing a technology program and the most valuable feedback should be from teachers since they work on the "front-lines" everyday. From an administrative viewpoint, it is crucial that professional development opportunities are in place for the teaching staff. I feel the "virtual tomatoes" flying at me now for the next statement I am about to make. In order for our students to get the most and learn the proper way to use the technology, our teachers must be trained. *Teachers, if we are not willing to adapt our teaching methods to meet the needs of our students, we are failing them.*

As previously addressed, Administrators need to be the visionaries of the technology or digital classroom program. Administrative involvement is another key factor in whether the technology program fails or succeeds. They need to be in constant contact with teachers to get necessary feedback to continue the development of the program. According to the report <u>Administrative Aspects of Technology Implementation in Special Education</u>, it was crucial for the program's success for administrators to provide centralized and decentralized leadership. For example, the report states, "several projects found value in this decentralization and the flexibility it allowed, advising administrators to encourage rather than force the use of technology (Author Unknown, 1992). Administrators also need to provide training and support to teachers before and during the implementation of the program. The report stated that teacher training was the most important factor in the success implementation of the technology program.

The "Look" of the Digital Classroom.

Taking into consideration that a "digital divide" exists not only within the U.S., but around the world, I will suggest a "low" budget or more affordable digital classroom. I could write and describe this state-of-the-art classroom that I would like to have, but in reality I know it is not possible. Currently, my classroom probably has the most technology within my building (except the computer labs) "minus" an interactive white board. I currently have an LCD projector, 5 computers with 256 ram (dinosaurs), a 2-year old laptop, 3-DV cameras, a Flipcam, and DVD/VCR combo. Ideally, it would be nice to have a one-to-one laptop program, but realistically as educators, we must do what we can with what we have. Another thing I am currently exploring is how to incorporate new mobile technologies, for example, the Ipod Touch and cellular phones.

So, what should the "affordable", "low-budget" digital classroom look like? I would incorporate the following items to create a digital classroom.

This is basic list and careful lesson planning would need to occur to keep all students engaged.

Here is a basic list with estimated costs for each:

LCD projector- It is possible to purchase one for $500 depending on brand and specifications. LCD projectors take the place of a bulky TV set and provides a "larger" screen for students to view videos and lecture material.

Laptop computer- Depending on brand and whether you want to go Mac v.s. PC, will determine the amount you spend. For a PC laptop, you could purchase one for less than $500. Mini laptops are around the $200 price range. With budget concerns, a mini laptop could be the way to go. Just be sure to check the specifications and watch the built in memory, some only come with 8 GB.

Open Source Software- a lot of software applications are relatively cheap and free. There are similar applications to Microsoft Word and other costly items. So instead of wrapping a considerable amount of your budget money into software, consider your options with open source software.

Flipcamera- A digital flip camera is the most affordable way to go with digital video. For about $150 you can get a good DV camera that downloads very quickly. They also make them with HD capabilities.

DVD/VCR- This can be plugged directly into the LCD projector. A DVD/VCR combo can now be purchased for less than $100.

These products are just a couple of suggestions to get started. Obviously, if money was not an issue, I would suggest an interactive white board, a mobile laptop lab, and a mobile Ipod Touch lab. These tools will be discussed as we discuss tools for teachers and students in later chapters.

The final element I want to discuss is the evaluation process of the digital classroom. As a classroom teacher, I constantly ask myself, are my students engaged? Are they getting the key concepts of what my objectives and goals were? What new tools would help them achieve and obtain the goals set forth? By evaluating the digital classroom plan or district technology plan, administrators can more accurately make decisions on how to improve the program. The evaluation process can prevent future problems, get needed training for teachers, and see what impact the technology is having in the classroom. The evaluation process must begin with the classroom teacher. A clear and measurable criteria is important to accurately determine the effectiveness of the digital classroom.

Teaching the correct way to use technological tools is the key to success for our children in the future. The teacher and the administrators need to be communicating to see that the technology/digital classroom program is a success. It is the administrator's role to see that the teachers are properly trained and that they have the resources they need to be successful. The most crucial aspect of a successful technology/digital classroom program is the planning and evaluation of the technology program. These three factors will determine whether a technology program succeeds or fails.

Chapter 7

Tools for Students in the Digital Classroom

Creativity requires the courage to let go of certainties—

Erich Fromm

Students today are "wired" a little different than I was or the generations of students before. It is amazing but students can play video games, text message, listen to their Ipod, watch TV, and type a paper all at the same time. Okay, so maybe I'm exaggerating a little, but children today are living in a multimedia driven world and can use many different tools/technologies at the same time. Their brains are constantly "switching" gears every 3-5 minutes. Our classrooms are a shock to their systems. They come from a technology and media-driven world to a classroom that is taught from a "one-dimensional" point of view. In some cases, we lose our students within a minute or two of them sitting at their desks in our classroom. So once they are lost, it is very difficult to keep them engaged. It is crucial that students engage within the first few moments of class. It is vital that they are able to apply the classroom to the outside world. In this chapter, I will discuss several tools our students own and how they can be used within the classroom setting.

Laptop/PC

Computers and the internet are becoming more and more affordable as technologies continue to develop. The ability to connect to the internet via "wifi" hot spots or internet cafes also gives our students access. My concern with laptop and pc use is the lack of students using them in productive and educational ways. Students have no problem finding the internet or pc games, but when asked to type a report or research something on the internet, they seem to be clueless. As educators, we need to assist them in using this valuable tool to prepare them for something they will do in the future. We (educators) understand and rely on computers, cellphones, etc., for a lot of our day-to-day operations. Wouldn't you think these skills are necessary for our students to learn and communicate, so they can be active and successful in today's society? Meaningful and life-changing assignments need to be given to our students instead of the daily, monotonous drill exercises they have become so accustomed to in our Mathematics and English classes.

      While discussing the access of computers and the internet within the home or access at libraries, school, and public cafes, I would like to explore the idea of the hybrid classroom. "Hybrid" includes an online element in addition to the face to face class meeting. I see each of my students approximately 45 minutes a day. A lot of those days there is not enough time to get a reading, writing, discussion, or grammar activity completed. With an online element involved, students could login at a convenient time and express their thoughts or concerns on the topic of the week. The idea is not to overwhelm them, but to provide a space for them to contribute. Have an active area for questions and basic thoughts in addition to a required area (one post per week).
Moodle is a great free online

classroom manager. Nings are also free online social networks. These are very user friendly. Moodle must be downloaded onto a server, where nings are completely web based. There are other open source web based course management systems available, but these are just two of my favorites.

Ipod/Ipod Touch

Whether it is the $60 shuffle or the $195 touch, or even a $25 mp3 player, each can be used as a tool in the classroom. Let's begin with the basic mp3 player or shuffle. With a basic pc, a free download from audacity (audio recording software), and a microphone, a simple podcast of your class can be recorded. For students who frequently miss or need a refresher come test time, this could be an awesome asset to your class. You may even ask students to create their own podcasts. One excellent way to do this is to have them do a podcast of their vocabulary terms. They will not only learn something, but this audio can now be placed online for download so others can use it to learn and review.

Now let's discuss the Ipod Touch. This is a wonderful tool for students to possess. There are hundreds of applications, not only for productivity, but also for homework assistance and help. Some of the applications cost a fee, but there are many that are free. The student must have "wifi" access to download the applications, but most are useable any time after the download. For example, dictionaries, quotes, writing tips, podcasts are available to assist students or provide additional learning opportunities. There are also applications that allow the user to send 15 text messages for free and for a small fee send unlimited. This is an alternative way to participate in the classroom activities that I will discuss in the cell phone section of this chapter.

In a lot of cases, lack of funds for computers and space limits the technology in schools. Some schools have invested in classroom sets of Ipods. As long as a wireless signal is available, each Ipod can function as a computer, which allows the student access to information at their finger tips. In addition to the web, students have access to a multitude of applications. For math class, a graphing calculator costs around $85. A 99 cent graphing calculator application gives students the same calculator on their Ipod touch. For social studies classes, there are a multitude of maps you can download, in addition to Google Earth. There are so many applications to discuss, it would take a whole book to describe. One thing is for sure, the Ipod touch has the potential to transform the classroom experience.

Cellular/Mobile Phones

3.3 billion....approximately 1/2 the population of the earth...have cell phones. The last two years I have been on the totally opposite side of the spectrum of the argument I am about to "endorse". Through research and my love of technology, I have begun to try and find a way to use cell phones as a tool within the classroom instead a banning or penalizing students for using them. In the past, I have seen them as a complete nuisance. On several occasions, I would take them from students if I saw them, since school policy required students to keep cell phones in their lockers. Our policy was that the phone would be locked up for 24 hours for the 1st offense, 48 hours for the 2nd. In fact, last year I collected nearly 40 cell phones from students texting when they shouldn't be. You are probably thinking, why embrace cell phones now? I'm asking how am I going to sell the idea to my administrator after being 100% anti-cell phone in the classroom? Cell phones are not going away. The texting and other applications available on phones today is relatively affordable. Information is literally at students' finger tips. Cell phones now can be used to shoot video as well. I honestly feel we as educators are "missing the boat", if we are not using the cell phone as a tool. What rules or policies need to be in place when using the cell phone as a tool within the classroom? What happens when a student "crosses the line"?

Cell phones provide multiple opportunities for students to engage within the classroom. A major debate rages about the use of cell phones. Some are 100% against like I was a year and a half ago, or are trying to find ways to use this valuable tool. Once the teacher has decided to adapt the cell phone as a tool, he or she must then sell their administrator on the idea since policy states they are not allowed. In order to implement a cell phone program within your classroom, each of the following must be considered. I will discuss the goal of the program, procedures, parent/teacher communication, discipline procedures for misuse, and the benefits of the program. Each of the following considerations is part of a plan I submitted to my administrator to ask for a "pilot" class in which I would use cell phones for part of the instruction. At the time of this writing, this is what I believe using the cell phone in the classroom would do. Unfortunately, I have no data at this time to show how cell phone instruction improves student motivation and engagement in the classroom.

The goal and purpose for cell phone instruction in the classroom is simple. Many teens have them and are using them, so why not teach them a positive productive way to use them. In the business world, million dollar deals are being closed with cell phones. My goal for classroom instruction is to create a classroom environment that fosters creativity, respect, and understanding. In the case of the classes I teach, 91% of my students own a cell phone with at least texting options. The class I am proposing to "pilot" test has 100% cell phone saturation. First and foremost, students need to see the value and the responsibility that comes with such an activity. Students need to understand that when a cell phone becomes an educational tool, the "senseless" (not having to do with the lesson) texting, and games cannot occur. Clear and precise procedures must be established. Depending on the activity (three activities will be discussed), students would be required to place their cell phone on the corner of their desk and only touch it when prompted by the teacher. Upon completing the prompted activity, students will be required to place their phone back in the corner of their desk. To some this already sounds like a nightmare. No, not really, because you as the teacher are walking around monitoring their activity, not sitting behind the desk reading the news and sports, or checking the email. The teacher must remain engaged with the students. This holds them accountable and makes your program work. Sounds fairly easy to implement, but clear rules and what is expected is crucial for success of this program.

    Another thing to consider when implementing a cell phone program with in your classroom is parental communication. One sure way to get your program "shut down" is by having a parent call, wondering why their son or daughter is 50 texts over and now owes several hundred dollars. The texting bill states that 50 texts took place between 12:45-1:30 on Monday, Tuesday, and Wednesday. Here is the solution have a meeting with the parents or send home a letter explaining your program. In order for the student to participate in the cell phone activity, they must have parental permission. Several applications I plan on using the cell phone with can also be found on the web. This provides an alternative to those who are unable to participate. Another way to get these students involved is to allow them to partner up with those that are able to use their cell phone. Depending on the size of your school or class, a parent meeting might be next to impossible, but would probably be the best way to "pitch" your program and get parental support. A letter explaining and a signature allowing their child to participate are important elements to have before you begin using cell phones in the classroom. It is very important that you discuss these forms with your students so they understand their importance. See a sample letter and form in the appendix (Appendix B & C).

Are you ready to implement your cell phone in the classroom project? I hope you are but there is one more thing you need to consider. What if a student disobeys or gets "off" task during the activity? What are the penalties? Were the penalties discussed in the parent note? Hopefully, the students understand that using a cell phone in the classroom is a privilege, not a right. Hopefully, they understand the responsibility as well. Before discussing possible penalties, let me make this statement: clear procedure must be in place when beginning a cell phone program. Below are a couple ways to handle a student who goes against the program criteria. Each is debatable and will be at the classroom teacher's discretion. Some may think the penalties are too light others too strict, these are only suggestions.

> 1) The student loses his privilege for the day and receives a failing grade for the day.
>
> 2) The student loses his privilege for the semester and has to participate in alternative assignments.
>
> 3) The student loses his privilege for the year and has to participate in alternative assignments.

It is crucial that students understand the severity of the penalties, in hopes that they will stay on task and complete the assignment to your standards.

I feel there are major benefits to implementing a cell phone program in your classroom. Most students that walk in my classroom own a cell phone, so why not utilize it. Opponents to cell phone use in the classroom argue that students will be distracted and off task. In years past and even today, teachers face the distraction of "note" passing. To prevent cell phones being a distraction, teachers must make clear procedures, especially if cell phones are not used on a daily basis. Cell phones have camera, video, and internet capability, in addition to their other functions and applications. One benefit that is probably not measurable, but vitally important to your classroom is student motivation and engagement. Instead of having students journal a response to a literary work, have them in 3-4 lines text you their response. Again, you as the teacher need to have pre-arranged criteria on the information you expect in the text. This not only engages each of the students, but allows them to use a tool that is usually banned with in the classroom. Another benefit to cell phones in the classroom, is the possibility of raising test scores. Again, this could be difficult to measure, but as we spend time reading test preparation material and students fill in the bubble sheets, cell phones/texting can provide an alternative. Using a free web-based application <u>Polleverywhere</u>, students can respond to the multiple choice test questions and the results will appear real-time. This will provide students will the opportunity to get prepared for a test, using 21st century technology. I also believe cell phones can aid in vocabulary development. Instead of the pencil and paper way of vocabulary, allow students to use their phones, the notepad option, or other application to record their vocabulary words. Through the use of the cell phone, they are engaged with the technology instead of the old pencil and paper way of vocabulary.

Another benefit to cell phones in the classroom is that it produces students to think critically and creatively. Cell phones could be used in filming (if the phone has video) or a picture slide show (if the phone as a camera). The teacher could assign students a world problem or another problem solving issue. Students would be required to put together a slideshow or short film with suggestions to solving it. If nothing else, students can learn the art of digital storytelling or understand another valuable use of the tool they carry everyday.

So, you have your plan and you are ready to implement. The plan is useless if the teacher sits behind the desk and doesn't get involved. This is crucial for successful implementation of a cell phone program. Another critical element is parental involvement. The final element is the school administration's "blessing". In a lot of schools, cell phones are banned to lockers or student's backpacks or pockets, turned off. The policy will have to be rewritten in a lot of cases. This is the typical policy: Students must have their phone turned off and not visible during school hours. Here is my amended policy that would allow cell phones to be used in the classroom: Students must have their phone turned off and not visible during school hours, UNLESS it is used under the supervision of a teacher for a classroom activity. Yes, this opens up some argument on what constitutes a "classroom activity". As I've stated throughout the chapter, setting a clear criteria and making sure students understand the magnitude of cell phones in the classroom will prevent most issues.

The three tools discussed in this chapter are good ways to get students engaged and using 21st century technologies. Most students have or own one of the tools, but usually do not use them for educational purposes. The issues surrounding cell phones in the classroom will continue to be debated. I hope that you take something you can apply to your classroom.

Chapter 8

Tools for Teachers in the Digital Classroom

Creativity is a type of learning process where the teacher and pupil are located in the same individual. –

Arthur Koestler

There is not enough time in our day. Our students are expected to perform on state standardized tests in addition to being ready to enter the global world. With the current state of education and NCLB mentality, how do teachers stay "on top of things" and share the knowledge needed with their students? In the pages that follow, I will discuss several tools as well as open source software solutions to increase productivity and decrease lesson preparation time.

The first tool is obvious, a pc or laptop computer. There are schools that do not have a computer in the classroom. This tool can transform the education process, even if there is only one computer. As discussed in the OER Promise and Inequality chapter, Sugata Mitra's "Hole in the Wall" experiment shows that students teach other students with one computer. A computer in the classroom can also be a major productivity tool for the teacher. Lesson planning, conducting research via the internet, enhancing lesson through the use of video via YouTube, TeacherTube, and other video websites will provide for a more engaging classroom. As computer prices and infrastructure becomes a little more affordable, our students may also continue to learn outside of the classroom based on demonstrations given by the teacher. For example, I came across a web based cartoon designer called *Toondoo* (http://www.toondoo.com). I demonstrated and created a "toondoo" representing a scene from Romeo and Juliet. The students were hooked. I had nine students out of fifteen who came in on a Monday stating they had created an account and began to design. This is possible due to the affordability of computers and access. My district is far from affluent, approximately 42% poverty.

    While discussing the idea of widespread pc in houses or access at cafes, I would like to explore the idea of the hybrid classroom. The hybrid classroom is a new concept I'm trying this year. This is also a very valuable tool for teachers to continue the lesson and discussion outside of class. I see each of my students approximately 45 minutes a day. A lot of those days there is not enough time to get a reading, writing, discussion, or grammar activities completed. With an online element involved, students could login at a convenient time and express there thoughts or concerns on the topic of the week. The idea is not to overwhelm them, but provide a space for them to anonymously contribute. Have an active area for questions and basic thoughts in addition to a required area (one post per week). What I am finding is that students are reluctant to use this "hybrid" classroom, unless there is a major grade attached. 90% + have a Facebook and Myspace account, they know how it operates. However, giving this opportunity will enhance your classroom discussions when it works and students participate. Another great benefit to the hybrid classroom is a paperless classroom. The "dog ate my homework" excuse no longer applies. This not only saves resources, but in the long run can save your district money. Moodle is a great free online classroom manager. Nings are also free online social networks. These are very user friendly. Moodle must be downloaded onto a server, where Nings are completely web based. There are other open source web based management systems available, but these are two of my favorites.

Another tool or option for educators is the multitude of information or free professional development opportunities on the Internet. As educators, there are times during the year that we just need recharge We become worn out and our idea bank has run dry. As I'm writing, I'm thinking to myself "dude, you're only a third year teacher, what's up with you? How can you already be frustrated?" Those who know me know that when I commit, like most educators, I give 120%. My students deserve the best, and if I don't deliver, it's my fault. My job is to do my best to prepare them for their lives now-- and after high school. This is a major responsibility. With that said, we can't beat ourselves up, but look for ways to be positive and improve. One way to do this is to build a professional learning community. This doesn't have to be a "professional" membership to some group or a conference but something informal. In the digital world, we have the ability to connect with thousands of other teachers via nings, discussion boards, blogs, and other online avenues. Everyone has the ability and should have the desire to become the best they can be. Our students deserve it. I encourage you to develop a professional learning or motivation plan. Start now! Below is my motivation/professional improvement plan using open source materials so there is no cost to me except for the equipment (iPod touch, Amazon Kindle, computer, Internet).

	Step one is to find websites or blogs to visit that encourage you or give you suggestions on how to improve what you do. When my idea bank is dry, I consult two nings that relate to my subject area, English, I find that they are encouraging and discuss real classroom issues. Alan Sitomer's "Book Jam" Ning (thebookjam.ning.com) connects you to educators who share challenges and suggestions to improve. Mr. Sitomer blogs almost daily and his insight and humor on what occurs in the classroom is encouraging and challenging. The "English Companion" Ning is managed by Mr. Jim Burke. (englishcompanion.ning.com). This ning is nearing 10,000 members and is a wealth of English teaching information. Like the "Book Jam" ning, the "English Companion" ning discusses "real" teacher issues that you don't learn about when you go to "teaching" school.

	For step two, I would check out Itunes University. You can download Itunes for free on a pc or mac. There are thousands of podcasts from hundreds of fields. You can learn about something in your field from many universities that post lectures on Itunes. Itunes U gives you the opportunity to listen to motivational and inspirational messages as well.

For step three, I encourage you to develop a five-year plan for learning and improving. This plan is about setting goals. Once it is developed, plan on "tweaking" it. Here is part of mine from three-years ago. Every December I sit down and write a new five year plan. I find that if you write goals down, you have a better chance at achieving them. A lot has changed for me in the last couple of years so I had to tweak 2009 a little.

> 2007- begin my first year of teaching and provide the best environment I can for my students. Find a teacher mentor that can provide insight, encourage me, and challenge me to be the best teacher I can be.
>
> 2008- continue teaching, pursue professional development opportunities in classroom management and pacing. Start looking for a graduate program.
>
> 2009- Begin Global Studies program at University of Illinois and apply what I learn to my classroom. Continue researching ways to engage students and seek professional development opportunities in technology and open source education.
>
> 2010- Graduate the Global Studies program and continue to challenge myself

and my students to think "outside" the box. Begin offering professional development opportunities to teacher discussing technology and teaching in a global world. I plan to seek professional develop on Administration and the process of decision making in that position.

My example is plain and simple. Set forth a couple of goals for yourself. If you don't meet them, change them. If your plans totally change, like mine did, go with the flow and change them again. Getting where you want to be is a process and it won't happen overnight and it won't happen if you do not set goals.

      As discussed in other chapters, open educational resources are a great supplement to the classroom. Open source software can be very useful as budgets for technology continue to shrink. Here are a couple free and useful open source and web based applications. One free and open source application is OpenOffice. OpenOffice (http://www.openoffice.org), a product of Sun Microsystems (Sun), who was purchased by Oracle in April, provides word processing, spreadsheet, presentation capabilities. This software is very comparable to Microsoft Office Suite. For schools without a technology budget, this software is great. For teachers without the expensive software, it provides a professional alternative. As I prepare to teach my creative writing class next semester, I stumbled upon Webspiration (http://www.mywebspiration.com).

Webspiration is a great tool used for brainstorming and organizing ideas. This application is completely web based and allows the user to save their organized chart and links it to a url for others to view. As resources become limited, this can be an alternative to students using paper to brainstorm. They may create a chart and email you the link to grade them. Open source education has potential and will change education.

Another tool that is gaining popularity is the Amazon Kindle. This is basically a digital reader, it can store multitudes of books, magazines, newspapers, pdf files, and word documents. Unlike reading on a computer screen, the Kindle is digital paper. It is easy on the eyes and has absolutely no glare. Along with the convenience of book storage, the Kindle offers digital book/multimedia prices. When a novel in hardback may cost $35, the kindle price will most likely be under $10. Not only does the Kindle offer readers a massive, cost-lowering storage device, it also includes global 3G. With Amazon, Wikipedia, and Google preloaded, the Kindle can look up directions, encyclopedia passages, foreign language translation, and email from anywhere, without a monthly subscription or contract. Amazon's 3G is completely free and included in the price of the device. Many universities are encouraging students to purchase the Kindle for their textbooks. We know how much weight students have to carry in the backpacks during school. Textbooks are heavy and expensive. Imagine carrying all of the books on a Kindle and paying approximately $10 a book. Even though the Kindle runs $250-500, it can be an extreme money saver for students and teachers.

Now, let's look at the final tool I will discuss, the iPod Touch. Awesome! Enough said. This is also a student tool that I discuss in the "Tools for Students" chapter. I purchased my touch a few weeks before my birthday and it has transformed my normal morning routines. Instead of waking up and sitting down at the computer, I can grab my touch, check the news and email as I walk to the shower. This cuts out about 15 minutes out of my routine. In fact, I'm currently writing this chapter at the fitness center while riding an exercise bike. I'm using a preloaded application called "notes". When I'm finished, I will simply email them, copy them from my email to a word processor, and make minor format changes. The touch has wireless internet capabilities, so anywhere there is wifi, it automatically finds it and uses it. Of course, some are pass coded, but I can find signal in most places. The Touch definitely keeps me connected.

Some people view iPods as toys for entertainment purposes, I view mine as a tool of productivity. There are hundreds of free applications. From news to weight loss to calendars and list makers, there is something for everyone. So, the touch plays a role in my everyday life, what about my professional/teacher life? There are many applications that deal with all subject areas. Maps for the social science teacher, all of Shakespeare's writing for the literature teacher, stoichiometry simulation for the chemistry teacher, pitch pipes for the music teacher, there is truly something to benefit every teacher. As I was researching applications for educators, I found several time saving and organizational applications. Teacher Tool One provides a grade book, notebook, course register, and provides a note for each student. It can also be a place to record student attendance. This application syncs with a mac or pc and is backed up each time you plug it into the computer. You can literally carry your grade book, course rosters, and notes on students in your pocket. Another useful application that would be useful for keeping lesson plans is myHomework. Designed for a student to keep track of classes and assignments, I feel it would be a great tool for a teacher to organize lesson plans. Some applications do charge a fee, but for the most part are completely free. You can often download the "lite" versions of any application with no charge. The touch literally provides teachers information at their finger tips. Various study guides or notes to novels are available for download.

There are many options for educators to use technology in the classroom. As technology becomes more affordable and accessible, teachers need to be able to instruct students on how to use it correctly. Through the use of the computer, the iPod Touch, the Amazon Kindle, and the multitude of opportunities open educational resources offer, education will be transformed. In addition to providing resources for our classrooms, these tools can provide opportunities for professional development and motivation. Each tool has the power to transform our lives as well as our students.

SECTION IV

The Future Of Education

Chapter 9

Teaching Individuality through the use of Open Educational Resources

Undoubtedly the hardest task of the educator is to help a growing youth to know himself, for that involves a wide knowledge of others. A boy has to learn to play his part with others, and not to live in solitude […] Allow some novel thoughts to grow without much criticism. If the soil is of the right sort and well cultivated, bad seeds will not take root, and only what is good will flourish there—

T.G. Rooper (1902).

This chapter seeks to look into and pose questions regarding education in the Open Resource movement. What benefits will the field of education receive from this new technology, and how must education change to create a fresher approach to pedagogy? Will the Cartesian model hold our attentions as we delve into the new millennium, or must we adapt to a more individualized approach to learning?

Perhaps the first issue to be addressed is why use the term Individualization in the age of Personalization. Personalization is much easier to identify and incorporate into large-scale projects. In the U.S.A. for instance, companies send mass mailings daily with an individual's name printed on the front of the envelope and in the header of advertisements. Do we accept this personalization as being made for us? Naturally, we know that it was not written specifically for the "individual." Instead, we toss it aside, rarely, if ever, to be seen, or read, again. The same happens online, through cookies and browsing preferences. Although this "tweaking of standardization" is more palatable than mass advertising, it still lacks a certain substance, which is requested in our modern age. It seems that the more technologically advanced we become, the more we cling to what is individualized. We want something written specifically for our needs or wants, not something of little substance or importance to us with our name tacked on the front.

According to George Ritzer, the globalization of nothing, meaning mass-produced chains or large corporations, is the only product capable of being globalized. Something, on the other hand, meaning quaint stores, mom and pop diners, etc., are merely local, because the relationships cannot be transported (Ritzer, 2007).

Is it possible, to export something education? Can education be made not only personal, but also geared solely for the individual? I argue, that Open Educational Resources can indeed bridge the gap between standardization and personalization, and furthermore from personalization to individualization. Not only will students be interested in personalized learning plans, but they will also be able to create their own individualized studies that will shape them into a unique individual, not just a standardized learner of rote information.

Education Past and Future

Education has been based on the Cartesian model for centuries. The Cartesian model embraces the idea that knowledge is a substance, and must be passed down from authoritative figure to student through learned teaching techniques and pedagogical theories. Many artists, singers, philosophers, and great thinkers have criticized the Cartesian model and our system of education. Since the time of T.G.

Rooper in 1902, people have realized that something in our schools needs to change. One of the most popular criticisms, is Pink Floyd's 70s hit song, "Another Brick in the Wall," based on the bass player, Roger Waters, and his experiences in the British school system. BBC Magazine's Denise Winterman explains, "It was a protest against the strict regime he felt had tried to suppress children, rather than inspire them" (Winterman, 2007). Is education merely numbing youths' ability to think critically and creatively, creating a myriad of students who accept knowledge without being able to discern the good from the bad? Will traditional education be able to sustain our eagerness for reform in the twenty-first century, or will new forms of education take hold? Through this chapter, I hope to show that education may evolve in the near-future due to the increase of Open Educational Resources (OER's) and the options they give for individualized study, global experiences, and building critical and creative thinking.

    Since the Middle Ages, European-based countries have used the same model for education. There are three sub-categories of school, Primary, Secondary, and Tertiary. In theory, teachers are trained to broadcast certain information, based on the sub-category, to every student in the same manner, always maintaining equality and standardization in all pupils. This model is based on solid principles, which have obviously withstood the test of time. It teaches young minds structure, respect for authority, diligence, equality, and patience for tedious work. However, unless a student falls within the category of "average," which I argue is fairly rare, this model bores, manipulates, or goes beyond the capabilities of many students. Furthermore, how can students begin to excel with their natural talents, when they are forced to compete on the same core-subjects as every other student? There is no room for individual growth before the Tertiary phase; therefore, there is no time for most students to truly excel before reaching adulthood.

    Are there ways to bring out natural talents in the traditional school setting? Back to the knowledge of T.G. Rooper in 1902, "in most cases these are of an average type, a common education and routine is both possible and desirable. The demand to have one teacher for one child is as false in theory as impracticable. We have, however, to be keenly alive to the exceptional types, and deal with these prudently" (Rooper, 1902). Should there then be one teacher to one student, if the student is "exceptional"? What does Rooper mean by "average type" and "exceptional"? I think that his idea here is the basic model of what dominated the twentieth century. The idea that, most students are the same, only a few differ, and they need special attention. There were no other ways to think about this issue, because, even if every student would be exceptional, there were no funds or resources available to personalize learning programs for millions of different students.

The basic curriculum had to apply to the majority. Beyond the lack of teachers or resources, the students' needs for education in their life were also different for the majority of the twentieth century. The work force was based on white-collar and blue-collar. The industries were either service or production. The opportunities for specialization were rare, if available at all. As technology improves, however, the work also changes drastically. "Technology and invention make some work obsolete, call for new work skills, and always seem to progress the country in the direction of more material comforts, a higher standard of living, and an improvement in the social and economic structures of the nation" (Applebaum, 1998, p. XIII) Because of these changes in the work force and the lifestyle, our education model needs to adapt to the new requirements of civilization. At this stage, with the technology that does most of the reading, writing, and arithmetic for us, should we still be focusing on these manual, core subjects? If the primary purpose of education is to train productive, working, and fulfilled citizens, education needs to become more open, personalized, and technologically advanced. We are doing our students a disservice by not adapting to fit their ever-expanding needs.

Yong Zhao, a Chinese-American Scholar, discusses what schools need to do to prepare students adequately to become competent citizens. He discusses in his "What Knowledge Has the Most Worth" article, that Indian engineers get paid less than 5 times what a company would have to pay an American. With the global market and transnational corporations, why then, would anyone hire an American worker? The answer lies in a so-called special "something:"

> [T]he right brain-directed (R-directed) skills (simultaneous, metaphorical, aesthetic, contextual and synthetic) are the new ones Americans should acquire because jobs that use the left brain-directed skills (sequential, literal, functional, textual and analytic) are being outsourced to Asia and machines. Correspondingly, the new essential aptitudes, Pink says, are design, story, symphony, empathy, play and meaning [...] The natural follow-up question is why we believe Americans can develop the R-directed aptitudes while the Chinese cannot. In fact, no such guarantee exists. China has been reforming its education system to cultivate creativity and the R-directed aptitudes. So, too, have other Asian countries, notably Japan, South Korea and Singapore. The United States, on the other hand, has been emphasizing the opposite. If NCLB and similar standardization efforts succeed, we may well lose the advantage in cultivating the right-brain aptitudes. Before the implementation of NCLB, the U.S.

education culture was more conducive to (or at least tolerant of) talents besides the sequential, literal and functional (Zhao, 2008).

The U.S.A. and other euro-based countries should be focusing more on individualization based on critical thinking and creativity to remain competitive in the Global Workforce.

Many countries have noticed these trends and attempted to adopt some form of personalization, if not individualization, in the classroom. England and Scotland are among these nations. According to Michael Peters, Professor of Global Education at University of Illinois:

> It might be argued that personalization is an idea whose time has come. In a very short period of time personalization came to define the British labour Government's political philosophy, social policy, and new style of molecular government. This shift was a response to modernizing social democracy in the face of increasing globalization and a new 'openness' characterized by digitalization of society (Peters, 2009).

The UK spent £1.3 billion on supplementing personalized education between 2006 and 2008. They are hoping to reach their reform goals by

2020, offering their students truly personalized learning.

Of course, this solution is not without it critics. Michael Peters continues to explain that this strategy presents a loss of "educational targets, obligatory testing of pupils, and publication of text results" (Peters, 2009). There would be no way to create a median for what is taught or learned if everyone is studying in a different direction. Civilization would lose common ground or common knowledge among its citizens. We must also equally consider the costs of remaining standardized, these costs can be found throughout this chapter, as well as the rest of this book.

Other models or ideas of reform have been created. One of those models is Participatory or Social Learning. This learning system functions best where students learn from each other, from other pupils around the world by simply participating in activities. It is the antithesis of the Cartesian Model. Students merely learn from participating with each other and the world. As John Seely Brown and Richard P. Adler explain, "By contrast, instead of starting from the Cartesian premise of 'I think, therefore I am,' and from the assumption that knowledge is something that is transferred to the student via various pedagogical strategies, the social view of learning says, 'We participate, therefore we are'" (Brown, J.S. & Adler, R.P., 2008).

This idea is also not without its criticisms. When students merely participate in a task to learn something, or people attempt the impossible without former training, it is likely to turn chaotic. Is there, then, a proper way to supply students with a more in-depth personalized learning system, without the major costs, loss of authority or of standardization?

Open Educational Resources (OERs)

Open Education is a concept, which may prove to be the long awaited answer. The idea that free and open education is available on any given topic at any given point of the day will offer the global community a new insight on how education can be perceived. One OER, Connexions, boasts on their website that they offer free educational modules, curriculum, and even courses for students and teachers alike. They claim that sharing information and knowledge should be a high priority in the future market. MIT's OpenCourseWare also accepts that authoritative knowledge should be shared with the masses. Wikipedia is another open resource that has gained wide and authoritative acceptance around the world, quickly overtaking Britannica as the most used Online Encyclopedia. However, students must not take P2P collaborations as absolute. Educators must teach students to be weary of all online sources and to "fact check" all information.

As OER's gain acceptance around the world, and slowly work their way into American classrooms, students will be given the opportunity to pick and choose what works best for their learning habits, and teachers will gain access to "mix and matching" their textbooks. As Rob Farber points out, "Students interested in self-instruction can pick and choose topics and video lectures at will from the Web, while instructors now have the ability to create their own textbooks from selected materials posted on the site" (Farber, 2009).

To further OER's and Internet learning in general, technology introduces Web 3.0. Web 3.0 offers much insight into the possibilities of upcoming trends in publishing, researching, and learning. Michael Jensen, the Director of Strategic Web Communication of the National Academies, writes:

> Most technophile thinkers out there believe that Web 3.0 will be driven by artificial intelligences – automated computer-assisted systems that can make reasonable decisions on their own, pre-selective, pre-clustering, and preparing material based on established metrics, while also attending very closely to the user's individual actions, desires, and historic interests and adapting to them (Jensen, 2007).

Research convenience will also flourish. Search engines will run on very specific and accurate word and context investigating. Anything will be within a laymen's ability to research, and nearly everything will be free and open. The computer will monitor the user's interests, and it will filter information geared on the specific concentrations of the user. General knowledge will evolve into very personalized, perhaps even obscure, subjects and topics. Furthermore, according to Richard Baraniuk, professor at Rice University and creator of Connexions, Connexions will adapt to Web 3.0 by adopting:

> An assessment system should either be constructed, integrated, or linked into the current Connexions architecture. Since many teachable moments arise when no instructor is present, Connexions should encourage student users to tutor each other. […] Connexions should provide spaces for students to collaborate on interactive, multimedia problems and projects—what John Seely Brown calls 'thinkering,' for thinking + tinkering. […] Connexions should experiment with artificial intelligence tools such as cognitive tutors. These software systems provide direct, immediate, and individualized feedback and instruction to students as they work on problems based on a cognitive model of their understanding and potential misconceptions of the material (Baraniuk, 2007).

Learning possibilities are nearly endless with technology of this caliber. The ability to gain resources and free-education would require no previous knowledge of research, it would be mindlessly easy.

Individualization is inevitable with OERs. The amount of information modules and courses available are nearly countless. Any topic ever considered can be discussed and shared with the masses, all free-of-charge. Programs of study will be able to be created and taught instantly based on the student's interests, capabilities, and current knowledge.

Web 3.0 translation models will also flourish, allowing information to be passed from country to country without language or cultural barriers. If, and when, OERs are accepted in the classroom, the class will automatically become a global experience because of the widespread content and the users from around the world. Students will be able to comment on modules and read other comments left by students of all ages, races, languages and ethnicities.

Critical thinking and creativity are other skills that OERs may develop or foster. With the ability to re-write the textbooks, or to create one's own, OERs will give students the opportunity to think towards the sharing of knowledge. Class projects may include creating modules or editing them. With these options, students will be forced to be creative and to think about their world critically. Complacency as citizens will not be an accepted trend when everyone, even students have the power to change their curriculum and the content therein.

Now perhaps the question is, will OERs one-day function like the classroom and guide students towards seeking answers and developing their skills without the help of a live educator? Could Artificial Intelligence overtake the need for the school-system? When students will be shown by their computers what they should learn, then tested on said information, finally being corrected by Artificial Intelligence tutors, the traditional school setting will have little to no importance in a young student's life. How will education maintain its quality and truth?

Projects like Wikipedia, with lenses and open editing, are a good example of how OERs will sustain themselves in the rapidly evolving information market. Wikipedia offers people an opportunity to democratize learning. The more an article or fact is debated, the more prestigious and authoritative it becomes. This is how Open Education plans to sustain and maintain quality control. Everything will be peer-reviewed. All essays and articles will have links to where they have been quoted, or used. Information will be scoured, and many people will share in writing the articles or lessons. There is one issue of sustainability that still puzzles me. How, assuming this over-takes modern education, will all of our current information, textbooks, and knowledge stay authoritative when anyone can write or change the information? What will keep eager teenagers, who know very little about any given subject, from over-powering the intellectuals in the knowledge of technology, therefore altering and changing the ultimate truths we have shared for hundreds of years. History will be even more constantly altered than it is now, and nothing will be totally sustainable. I see it working as well as the game of "Telephone." One person has and writes the ultimate truth, and then twenty years later the original truth has been passed through hundreds of new writers and what parts of the original still exist? I argue, not very few. The same situation applies to textbooks and lectures, but there are not as many people with the authority or ability to publish as what the OE movement is offering.

Conclusion

I believe that the OE movement supplements education and educators beautifully. However, I do not agree with the motive of some activists who think that OERs will replace schoolroom education. There are still so many lingering questions regarding OERs and the inequalities therein (see our chapter "OERs Promise and Inequality for more on this). I think, however, that they could be used toward the reform of the school system. Teachers should utilize these resources to aid in individualizing their classrooms and offer their students ideas for independent study and research. Under the supervision of the school and parents, students should be able to foster their natural talents through study, playing, and as John Seely Brown states, "thinkering" with these sources online. Educators and education centers probably won't become endangered in the next century; however, I see the OE movement spreading throughout the world and offering personalization and unity for the global world simultaneously. If people will continue to share their knowledge and their personal talents generously with the help of OERs, we may not end the need for school, but rather achieve a more complex goal of unifying the world through the gift of education.

Chapter 10

The Promise of OERs and The Inequalities that Exist

The children of the rich get a different education than the children of the poor. We continue to fight that battle every way we can-

Arne Duncan (U.S. Education Secretary)

In our global world, technology is changing at a very rapid pace. Industrialized countries are thriving. Developing countries are improving, but not at the same pace as the industrialized nations. Educational opportunity also varies from state to state and country to country. Open Educational Resources provide an opportunity for teachers and students to have access to new information and new materials almost instantaneously. Unfortunately, some students within the United States will have greater opportunity due to the access of technology that is not available to all. Not that all inequality is caused by racial and ethnic background, but this is what the data shows. "Of the 51 poorest districts in Illinois, more than half are majority-black. Three out of four African-American children and two thirds of Latino children in Illinois attend school in a high-poverty district" (Lockette, 2009). In a Washington Post interview, former Chicago Public Schools CEO and Department of Education Secretary Arne Duncan made the following comment on the education situation in Illinois, specifically the Chicago Public Schools. "It is totally separate and totally unequal". "The children of the rich get a different education than the children of the poor. We continue to fight that battle every way we can" (Lydersen, 2008). Will these students have access to open educational resources? Will they be left behind? Can open educational resources provide opportunities for these students and transform their educational experience? The same questions need to be asked with students in developing countries.

Many challenges face the education system worldwide. According to PBS Frontline, "less than 5 percent of computers connected to the Internet are in developing countries" ("The hole in," 2002). What obstacles or challenges do open educational resources bring? Without access to the technologies in which OERs can be accessed the non-affluent students do not have the same opportunity as affluent students, thus the gap between affluent and non-affluent will grow. It is important to note the problem is with existing inequalities, not with open educational resources.

Before discussing open educational resources and their impact on education, it would be beneficial to define the term and its background. In 2002, United Nations Educational Scientific and Cultural Organization (UNESCO) defined open educational resources (OERs) as "technology enabled, open provision of educational resources for consultation, use, and adaptation by a community of users for non-commercial purposes" ("Iterating," 2006). Several examples of open educational resources are: wikis, online lecture material, blogs, and experiments that are recorded on video. The idea of openness can be expressed in this quote by Albert Einstein, "If you give a penny, you will be one penny richer and I'll be one penny poorer. But if I give you an idea, you will have a new idea, but I shall have it too." Einstein's quote identifies the belief that if knowledge is shared, ideas will still be with the person generating the idea, but also new ideas for other people. People can

transform the idea and make it their own transforming the idea and then passing it on to more people.
Current State of Education

Open educational resources have the potential to change the world of education. In industrialized nations, the potential is much larger due to the technology, infrastructure, and other resources. While OERs have potential, it also is important to note inequalities already exist within education. In order for OERs to benefit education countries need to reduce poverty, provide adequate educational funding, provide reliable internet access, and invest in technology infrastructure. The expense of textbooks is a small fortune. In some districts within the U.S. textbooks are either old or non-existent. According to Barbara Kurshan, "the Education Divide is caused by the mounting cost of textbooks, curricula, and other learning materials, which makes it difficult for communities with limited financial resources to provide their children with quality education" (Kurshan, 2007). She also alludes to the fact that education should be accessible to all, not just those with money. Those that believe OERs will change education for all argue that money could be used for technology infrastructure. If textbooks and basic operation costs cannot be covered, there is a possibility the money will not be used on technology infrastructure or computer systems. If the education divide exists without technology and open educational resources, how will open educational resources bridge the gap between the have and the have-nots?

OERs Benefits and Opportunities

Before exploring the challenges and how the gap could be bridged, let's focus on the benefits and opportunities of open educational resources. The effects of open educational resources could change education. "The ramifications of the OER effort are potentially huge, since individuals from around the world will have access to quality educational materials at any time over the internet—free of charge" (Farber, 2009). With open educational resources, educational information is at our fingertips. There is so much information out there. It is mind numbing.

Through wikispaces, nings, and other online social networks, teachers are able to collaborate and communicate to share information. The development of Moodle provides an excellent way to communicate and collaborate for our class. Connexions provides the learner with modules based on the subject matter they want to study. Connexions also works with other companies to provide educational material for no or low costs. "Non-profit Connexions' partnership with for profit QOOP (qoop.com) enables the production of print-on-demand paper textbooks that sell for a fraction of the price of commercial publisher" (Baraniuk and Burns, 2008). Another benefit to OERs is that they promote lifelong learning. For many people, being able to read and study at their own pace is a benefit and a lot of times you learn something. The internet and specifically open educational resources provides free information 24/7. Due to UNESCO's leadership in the OER movement, electronic versions of British medical journals were made accessible to developing countries (Johnstone, 2005). As an educator, open educational resources provide more flexibility in my lessons and planning of the lessons. On any given day, a person can visit my classroom and see every type of learning style take place, from audio to visual, to hands-on. It happens because OERs are available. The developers of open educational resources have all people in mind. It is admirable in a money driven society people are willing to share to help the less affluent. "A major reason for sharing resources created for local communities is individuals' desire to make a difference in the lives of those less fortunate" (Johnstone, 2005).

Challenges facing OERs

Open educational resources indeed have the potential to transform education as we know it. They also provide opportunities for developing countries. Unfortunately, many of the developing countries are being left behind technologically, thus a gap or digital divide is growing between the developed and the developing countries. According to the OECD Glossary of Statistical Terms, digital divide is defined as "the gap between individuals, households, businesses and geographic areas at different socio-economic levels with regard to both their opportunities to access information and communication technologies (ICTs) and to their use of the Internet for a wide variety of activities" ("Giving knowledge for," 2007). The divide exists for a variety of reasons including, but not limited to: extreme poverty, the lack of education funding, the lack of reliable internet access, and technology infrastructure. Although different, these reasons for the digital divide can intertwine.

Extreme poverty is one of main reasons the digital divide exists. In India alone, some 350 million people are living on less than a dollar a day ("The hole in," 2002). The quality of education is obviously lower in these developing countries. This lack of education leads to "over 800 million adults, two-thirds of whom are women—still lack basic literacy" (Suoranta and Vadén, 2009). With the lack of basic literacy, I'm proposing that it will be difficult for these 800 million adults to benefit from what OERs offer. Suoranta and Vaden also discuss this difference between the "North" and the "South" and depending on where you live, a person can have a better chance at a quality life. "By North and South, we refer to the economic, social, and educational gulf prevailing at the moment. In the South, people die of malnutrition, whereas in the North the most common cause of death result from being overweight" (Suoranta and Vadén, 2009). This comparison makes a valid point. There is a major and a distinct difference between the developed and the developing countries. We must be careful not to focus on the differences between the "North" and the "South". Focusing on the differences and not the commonalities leads to inequality.

This discussion of inequality in educational opportunities leads to a difficult and debatable question. Does education have to look the same for someone in a poor rural village and someone in a country who has all the resources to access technology and open educational resources? In developing countries, people are struggling with meeting their basic needs of food, shelter, and clothing. Within the inner cities of America, children are afraid of the violent and insufficient neighborhoods where they live. In the rural areas of developing countries as well as in America, children face poverty and other problems. Should education be individualized for people based upon the area in which they live? Is learning the basic information to survive in your culture an adequate enough education? Through Dr. Mitra's "Hole in the Wall Experiment", one can see how children are able to learn the basics of computing rather quickly. Dr. Mitra uses the term minimally invasive education to describe the process in which children can teach themselves without the supervision of adults. Minimally invasive education puts learning totally into the children's hands. "MIE uses children's natural curiosity and focuses on providing an enabling environment where they can learn on their own. Children, in the process of freely experimenting with the

Learning Station, pick up critical problem solving skills" (Hole in the," 2006).

Above we discussed the benefits of OERs. We briefly looked at the challenges and how the gap between the affluent and non-affluent, developed and developing countries continues to grow. How can this gap be bridged? "No single concept or project can possibly solve all the problematic issues afflicting people all over the world, but increasing educational options can help people help themselves" (Johnstone, 2005). One thing is for sure, the task will be difficult, but people are searching for ways to help. Robert Kennedy once said, "There are those who look at things the way they are, and ask why... I dream of things that never were, and ask why not? Several people have dreamed and are making those dreams reality. This is exactly what Nicholas Negroponte is doing with the One Laptop per Child Project. Internet cafes are now becoming realities in developing countries, allowing the common person access to the internet. Another major issue that could help bridge this gap is if developed countries would invest in the developing countries. In India, Dr. Sugata Mitra is doing his part at reducing the digital divide with the "Hole in the Wall Experiment".

The One Laptop per Child Project (OLPC) is a wonderful opportunity to put computers and technology into the hands of students in developing countries and even developed countries. Their mission is clear and well developed. "The mission of One Laptop per Child (OLPC) is to empower the children of developing countries to learn by providing one connected laptop to every school-age child. In order to accomplish our goal, we need people who believe in what we're doing and want to help make education for the world's children a priority, not a privilege" ("One laptop per," 2009). Until recently, people in the United States could not buy a $100 laptop. In 2007 and 2008, OLPC started the buy one get one program. One laptop would be sent to the buyer and the other would be sent to a country of the buyer's choice for $399. From a United States perspective, we have very impoverished districts that have few computers for their entire school. The schools in the suburbs are exposing their students to the OER technology, thus creating or growing a learning gap between the affluent and the non-affluent. The OLPC could close the gap in the United States because of the existing infrastructure. Another limitation to the OLPC Project is that governments have to buy in to the program. The common person cannot obtain one for their personal use. According to the OLPC Webpage, "the laptops are sold to governments to be distributed through the ministries of education with the goal of distributing "one laptop per child" ("One laptop per," 2009). The One Laptop per Child Project has potential to close the gap, but I feel it needs to reconsider its distribution model. As I was browsing the list of participating countries, many countries in Sub-Saharan Africa were absent, or there were less than 20,000 computers going into certain countries. This is alarming. If there isn't an equal and widespread distribution, I feel the gap between affluent and non-affluent will continue to grow, even in developing countries.

Another possible way to bridge the gap in the digital divide is the installation of internet cafes in developing countries. In Tanzania, a major increase in internet users has occurred due to internet cafes. Internet cafes provide computers and networking infrastructure to give patrons access to the internet and open educational resources. According to Furuholt and Kristiansen (2007), between 2000-2005 internet usage went from 60,000 to 333,000 users, a 455% increase in Tanzania. In the case of Tanzania, the data is showing there are more internet cafes in rural Tanzania than urban areas, which is creating a gap between rural and urban. Overall, I believe internet cafes can reduce the gap, however there are concerns. The main obstacles of maintaining and sustaining internet cafes are a combination between financial and political. Internet cafes usually charge a fee by the minute or hour making access limited to those who can afford access.

The "Hole in the Wall Experiment" by Dr. Sugata Mitra has the potential to bridge the technology gap. The "Hole in the Wall Experiment" began outside Mitra's office in the slum of Kalkaji, New Dehli, India, in 1999. Mitra placed a computer, connected to the internet, in a kiosk outside his office for anyone to use. "This computer proved to be an instant hit among the slum dwellers, especially the children. With no prior experience, the children learned to use the computer on their own" ("Hole in the," 2006). Since Mitra's initial experiment in 1999, he has set up additional experiments in other rural areas within the country of India. With its partnership with the International Finance Corporation, NIIT formed the Hole In The Wall Education Ltd, which will focus on putting computer kiosks in low-income areas around the world. Through the development of partnerships, more technology could be made available, thus increasing the effectiveness of OERs.

Conclusion

Our world is rapidly changing. Do OERs hold the answer to equaling the "playing field" between the affluent and non-affluent? Do open educational resources hold the key to closing the educational and digital divide? The challenges of open educational resources are substantial, but have the potential to be overcome. Progress is being made in the challenges of extreme poverty, lack of funding, lack of technology infrastructure, and lack of investment, at a very slow pace. Investment globally and locally has benefited some developing countries in getting access to the internet and OERs. Internet cafes have been a major factor in increasing internet usage in Tanzania. The One Laptop Per Child Project is an excellent start in equaling the playing field.

Dr. Sugata Mitra believes "computers can bring prosperity to poor, rural areas and provide local jobs" *(Digital Divide,* 2002). The problem that arises is only "some" people benefit leaving others behind. While great strides are being made to reduce inequality, I believe the gap between the poor and rich, affluent and non-affluent, developed and developing countries will continue to grow. Open Educational Resources and their effect will reach a small percentage of the population unless countries make a conscientious effort to reduce poverty, fund education properly, and invest in technology infrastructure, which includes reliable internet access. If these obstacles can be overcome, OERs have the great potential to change the world of education and provide opportunities to all.

APPENDIXES

Appendix A

Multimedia Projects and Ideas for Creativity

After years of the inability to create, students may need a push from their educators to understand this specific skill. Creativity cannot be taught, but it can be killed, as discussed throughout this book. By the time a student reaches high school it may be too late. The only way to overcome this fate is to practice creative thinking. There are many tools one can use to help spawn creativity. The list below are just a few of the options available.

The Book Report Sandwich Station is offered by Scholastic and is a free online program to help students have fun while learning about how to assemble a book report. It can be found here:

http://www.scholastic.com/kids/homework/sandwich.asp

For younger students **Imaginary City** is a fun tool to explore creativity and problem solving offered by Tate Kids. Here students can build their own cities, and you can discuss possible problems/outcomes of their innovations and structures.

http://kids.tate.org.uk/games/my-imaginary-city/

MIT has created a myriad of OERs and tools for students. One of their newest is called **Scratch**. This freeware downloadable program offers students the ability to write their own programming codes and easily create multimedia projects. Once created, these projects can be viewed online.

http://scratch.mit.edu/

ReadWriteThink also offers a lot of materials to students and teachers. Here one can find lesson plans, games, tools, and outside web resources. Students can find tools to create book covers, comics, postcards, riddles, crossword puzzles and much more.

http://www.readwritethink.org

For schools that have the ability to purchase programs and software, the options are nearly endless. For a great multimedia project creator look into **MediaBlender.** This program can be installed for as little as $50.00 along with nominal maintenance fees.

With the luxury of having a server, schools can create their own **Moodle** pages as well. This Open Source program is free and easily programmable by educators and staff. Here teachers can post forums, YouTube videos, **Sloodles**, and important documents. **Wiki**

Spaces and **Nings** provide similar spaces and are extremely user-friendly.

Literally any tool for the classroom can be found online. The world is accessible to our students, our classroom, and our schools, we just have to apply a little effort.

Appendix B

Letter To Parents

Dear Parent(s)/Guardian(s),

The students in my classroom are in the process of beginning a project that will help them connect the curriculum to the real world. I have enclosed a copy of the project for you to review. Thanks to our administration, we now have the ability to enhance your child's education by implementing the use of cellular technology in the classroom. Cell phones are one of most powerful communication devices on the globe. They provide students with a vast, diverse, and unique set of resources. The District's goal in providing this service is to promote educational excellence by facilitating resource sharing, innovation, and communication. Your authorization is needed before your child may use this resource.

With this educational opportunity also comes responsibility. You and your child should read the enclosed *Acceptable Use Policy (AUP)* and discuss it together. For your convenience, I have highlighted the section regarding the use of cellular technology (cell phones). Inappropriate material use may result in the loss of the privilege to use this resource. Remember that you are legally responsible for your child's actions. Ultimately, parent(s)/guardian(s) are responsible for setting and conveying the standards that their child or ward should follow. To that end, the School District supports and respects each family's right to decide whether or not to authorize your child to use cellular technology in the classroom. Before signing the authorization plan, please review your cellular agreement with your carrier. The district is not responsible for any costs that your child incurs while participating in this project or while at school.

Please read and discuss the *Acceptable Use Policy* with your child. If you agree to allow your child to use the cell phone for this project, please sign the *Authorization* form and return it to your school.

Sincerely,

Your Name Here

Authorization to Participate

(Required:)

I have read this *Acceptable Use Policy*. I understand that my child will be allowed to use his or her cell phone in class to participate in a classroom assignment, and that access is designed for educational purposes. I understand that the instructor will communicate the goals and objectives of the project to my child and the rest of the class. The instructor will also supervise the use of technology in the classroom during the project. However, I also recognize it is impossible for the District and the instructor to assume responsibility for my child's actions. I will hold harmless the District, its employees, agents, or Board members, for any harm or expenses incurred by inappropriate use. I accept full responsibility for supervision if and when my child's use is not in a school setting. I have discussed the terms of this *Authorization* with my child. I hereby request that my child be allowed to utilize his or her cell phone for the specific educational purposes outline by the teacher for the classroom project.

_____

PARENT/GUARDIAN NAME *(Please Print)*:_____

Signature:_____
Date:_____

Appendix C

Cell Phone Plan Survey

It is important to make sure that you have access to all the necessary tools before beginning any large project. Your assignment is to sit down with one of your parents and conduct a quick survey of your cellular plan. This will enable us to ascertain whether your plan provides you with the capability to use your phone during this assignment. This a graded assignment. Make sure to return the signed form by the assigned date. This form must be completed and signed by a parent or guardian before you will be allowed to use your phone in class.

1. Name your current cellular provider.
   _____

2. How many minutes are you allotted per month?
   _____

3. Does your plan provide for any free minutes?

   ☐ Yes ☐ No

4. If yes, use the area below to explain the plan in greater detail.

5. Does your current plan provide for unlimited texting?
   ☐ Yes ☐ No

6. If not, how many minutes are you allotted per month? _____

7. Does your phone have a camera?
   ☐ Yes ☐ No

8. If yes, how many megapixels is the camera?
   _____

9. Can you record video on your camera?
   ☐ Yes ☐ No

10. Explain the process you use to download media from your camera to a computer.

11. Do you have any questions or concerns about allowing your child to use his or her phone as a part of this assignment? If so, please provide a phone number or an email address where I can contact you.

Student Name:_____
                                            (PLEASE PRINT)

Parent Signature:_____

Date:_____

Student Grade:_____

Bibliography

<u>Chapter One:</u>
<u>Brief Introduction to the Millenial Generation</u>

Carr, Nicholas (2008). "Is Google Making Us Stupid." The Atlantic. http://www.theatlantic.com/doc/200807/google Accessed: 01/14/10.

Greenberg, E. & Weber, K. (2009). "Generation WE: how the millennial generation is taking over America and changing the world." Earthdaynetwork. http://ww2.earthday.net/generationwe. Accessed: 10/08/09.

Grossberg, L. (2005). Caught in the Crossfire: Kids, Politics, and America's Future. Boulder: Paradigm Publishers.

Oblinger, D. (2003). "Boomers, gen xers & millennials: understanding the new students." Educause. July/August. http://net.educause.edu/ir/library/pdf/ERM0342.pdf. Accessed: 10/08/09.

Sheahan, P. (2006). Gen Y: Thriving and Surviving with Generation Y at Work. Melbourne: Hardie Grant Books.

Textor, K. (Producer) (2008). "The millennials are coming." 60 Minutes. New York: CBS News.

"Understanding millennials." (2009) Making it Count! Educators. http://www.makingitcount.com/educators/article/view.asp?articleID=200. Accessed: 10/08/09.

<u>Chapter Two:</u>
<u>An In-Depth Look at Students Today Youth Culture: The New "Other"</u>

Bauman, Z. (2000). *Liquid Modernity.* Cambridge: Polity Press.

Chansanchai, A. (2006). Millennials lead the wired life. *MSNBC.* http://www.msnbc.msn.com/id/14560871/. Accessed: 10/22/09.

Ferguson, A. A. (2000). *Bad Boys: public schools in the making of black masculinity.* Lansing: University of Michigan Press.

Giroux, H. (1996). *Fugitive cultures: race, violence, and youth.* New York: Routledge.

Grant, J. (2004). The medicated generation. TEENAGERS: the millennial generation. http://www.wksu.org/news/features/adolescence/story/09. Accessed: 10/20/09.

Greenberg, E. & Weber, K. (2009). "Generation WE: how the millennial generation is taking over America and changing the world." Earthdaynetwork. http://ww2.earthday.net/generationwe. Accessed: 10/08/09.

Grossberg, L. (2003). Cultural studies, the war against kids, and the re-becoming of U.S. modernity. Postcolonial Studies. 6:3, 327-350.

Grossberg, L. (2005). Caught in the Crossfire: Kids, Politics, and America's Future (Cultural Politics and the Promise of Democracy). Boulder: Paradigm Publishers.

Harcombe, D. (2009). Marriage in a disposable society? *FAMILY.* http://marriage.families.com/blog/marriage-in-a-disposable-society. Accessed: 10/22/09.

Leyden, P. & Teixeira, R. & Greenberg, E. (2007). The progressive politics of the millennial generation. *New Politics Institute: a think tank for politics.* http://www.newpolitics.net/node/360?full_report=1 . Accessed: 10/26/09.

Oblinger, D. (2003). "Boomers, gen xers & millennials: understanding the new students." Educause. July/August. http://net.educause.edu/ir/library/pdf/ERM0342.pdf. Accessed: 10/08/09.

Peters, M. A. and Besley, A. C. (2006). Building Knowledge Cultures: Education and Development in the Age of Knowledge Capitalism. Lanham: Rowman and Littlefield Publishers, Inc.

Postman, N. (1992). *Technopoly: The Surrender of Culture to Technology.* New York: Vintage Books.

Ritzer, G. (2007). *The Globalization of Nothing 2.* Thousand Oaks: Pine Forge Press.

Sennett, R. (1998). *The Corrosion of Character.* New York: W.W. Norton & Company, Inc.

Sheahan, P. (2006). Gen Y: Thriving and Surviving with Generation Y at Work. Melbourne: Hardie Grant Books.

Spring, J. (2007). A New Paradigm for Global School Systems: Education for a Long And Happy Life. Mahwah: Lawrence Erlbaum Associates, Inc., Publishers.

Taylor, J. (n/d). Red flag: conditional love. *Parenting Bookmark.* http://www.parentingbookmark.com/pages/ACHV02.htm. Accessed: 10/22/09.

"Teaching The Millennial Generation" (2006). Knowledge@Emory. http://knowledge.emory.edu/article.cfm?articleid=956. Accessed: 01/14/10.

Textor, K. (Producer) (2008). "The millennials are coming." 60 Minutes. New York: CBS News.

"Understanding millennials." (2009) Making it Count! Educators. http://www.makingitcount.com/educators/article/view.asp?articleID=200. Accessed: 10/08/09.

Urycki, M. (2004). Status and coolness. TEENAGERS: the millennial generation. http://www.wksu.org/news/features/adolescence/story/07. Accessed: 10/20/09.

Chapter Three:
Fostering a Cosmopolitan Student In a World of Tests, Extreme Capitalism, and Cross-Cultural Comparisons

Bauman, Z. (2000). *Liquid Modernity.* Cambridge: Polity Press.

Ending Reaganomics. (2009). *Blackstate.* http://blackstate.com/endingreaganomics1009.html. Accessed: 10/29/09.

Hall, S. (2006). Cosmopolitan promises, multicultural realities. *Divided Cities: The Oxford Amnesty Lectures.* Oxford: Oxford University Press.

Hall, S. (2006). Interview of Stuart Hall. *YouTube.* http://www.youtube.com/watch?v=fBfPtRaGZPM. Accessed: 09/24/09.

Herndon, T. (1981). Is public education a casualty of Reaganomics. *New York Times.* http://www.nytimes.com/1981/11/15/education/is-public-education-a-casualty-of-reaganomics.html. Accessed: 10/29/09.

Nussbaum, M. (2008). Education for profit, education for freedom.

http://auroraforum.stanford.edu/files/essays/Nussbaum_Educ_for_Profit_Freedom.pdf. Accessed: 6/22/09.

Nussbaum, M. (1997). Capabilities and human rights. *Fordham Law Review*. No. 66. http://learn.ed.uiuc.edu/mod/resource/view.php?id=39479. Accessed:06/19/09.

Nussbaum, M. (1994). Patriotism and cosmopolitanism. *The Boston Review*. http://www.bsos.umd.edu/gvpt/theory/Patriotism%20and%20Cosmopolitanism.pdf. Accessed: 06/19/09.

Ritzer, G. (2007). *The Globalization of Nothing 2*. Thousand Oaks: Pine Forge Press.

Scott, C. (2006). Education and cosmopolitanism: a counterargument of Martha Nussbaum's assertion that U.S. students need an education based in cosmopolitan ideology. Associated Content. http://www.associatedcontent.com/article/36322/education_and_cosmopolitanism_a_counterargument.html?cat=9. Accessed: 06/19/09.

Sennett, R. (1998). *The Corrosion of Character*. New York: W.W. Norton & Company, Inc.

Spring, J. (2007). *A New Paradigm for Global School Systems: Education for a Long And Happy Life*. Mahwah: Lawrence Erlbaum Associates, Inc., Publishers.

Zhao, Y. (2008). What knowledge has the most worth. *The School Administrator.* http://www.aasa.org/SchoolAdministratorArticle.aspx?id=6032&terms=zhao. Accessed: 10/19/09.

Zhao, Y. (2009). What knowledge is of the most worth: education for the global economy. *Michigan State University.* http://www.verona.k12.wi.us/uploaded/Central_Office/Intranet/YongZhao.pdf. Accessed: 10/29/09.

Chapter Four:
Pitfalls to Standardized Testing: Falling Behind in the World

Au, W. (2005, Summer). No Child Left Untested: Small is Volatile. *Rethinking Schools, 19*(4). Retrieved from http://www.rethinkingschools.org/archive/19_04/vola194.shtml

Boutelle, M. (2009, June 22). The why of pie: Critical thinking makes mincemeat of fuzzy logic. *California Schools Magazine.* Retrieved from http://www.csba.org/NewsAndMedia/Publications/CASchoolsMagazine/2009/Summer/InThisIssue/CriticalThinking.aspx

Cress, J. (1974). Cognitive and personality testing use and abuse. *Journal of American Indian Education*, 13(3), Retrieved from http://jaie.asu.edu/v13/V13S3cog.html

Cronin, J. (2008, April). *The Impact of the No Child Left Behind Act on Student Achievement and Growth: 2005 Edition.* Retrieved from http://www.nwea.org/sites/www.nwea.org/files/NCLBImpact_2005_Study_0.pdf

Four Pillars of NCLB. (n.d.). *U.S. Department of Education.* Retrieved November 2, 2009, from http://www.ed.gov/nclb/overview/intro/4pillars.html

Illinois Kids Count 2009: Education for the 21st Century. (2009, January). *Voices for Illinois Children.* Retrieved September 25, 2009, from http://www.voices4kids.org/library/KC09_education.html

Jimerson, L. (2003, October). *Special challenges of the "No Child Left Behind" act for rural schools and districts.* Retrieved from National Educational Writers Association website: http://www.ewa.org/docs/rural.pdf

Kersting, K. (2003, September). Pondering high-stakes tests. *Monitor on Psychology, 34*(8). Retrieved from http://www.apa.org/monitor/sep03/pondering.html

Kohn, A. (2007, May 31). NCLB: Too destructive to salvage. In *Common Dreams.* Retrieved October 21, 2009, from Common Dreams website: http://www.commondreams.org/archive/2007/05/31/1558

Langenfeld, K. (1997). High Stakes Testing for Students: Unanswered Questions and Implications for Students with Disabilities. In *National Center on Educational Outcomes* . Retrieved October 11, 2009, from http://www.cehd.umn.edu/nceo/OnlinePubs/Synthesis26.htm

Peterson, K. (2005, July 7). NCLB goals and penalties. In *Stateline*. Retrieved September 20, 2009, from http://www.stateline.org/live/ViewPage.action?siteNodeId=136&languageId=1&contentId=41611

Renner, A. (n.d.). *Classism and education: NCLB, Regulated Knowledge, and Resistance*. Retrieved from http://www rohan.sdsu.edu/~rgibson/rouge_forum/renner.htm

Silva, E. (2008). *Measuring Skills for the 21st Century* [Data file]. Retrieved from http://www.educationsector.org/usr_doc/MeasuringSkills.pdf

Special Analysis 2009 International Assessments--How Do U.S. Students Compare With Their Peers in Other Countries? (n.d.). *National Center for Educational Statistics*. Retrieved October 23, 2009, from http://nces.ed.gov/programs/coe/2009/analysis/section1.asp

Chapter Five:
The Digital Classroom: Why and What it Looks Like

Author Unknown. Administrative Aspects of Technology Implementation in Special Education. A Synthesis of Information from Eight Federally-Funded Projects., 1992. http://www.eric.ed.gov/ERICDocs/data/ericdocs2sql/content_storage_01/0000019b/80/12/d2/a6.pdf

Boyd, Danah. (2007) "Why Youth (Heart) Social Network Sites: The Role of Networked Publics in Teenage Social Life." MacArthur Foundation Series on Digital Learning—Youth, Identity, and Digital Media Volume (ed. David Buckingham). Cambridge, MA: MIT Press

Lenhart, A (2007). Teens and Social Media. *Pew Internet and American Life Project*, Retrieved from http://www.pewinternet.org/

Mills, Steven, C. Integrating Computer Technology in Classrooms: Teacher Concerns When Implementing an Integrated Learning System., 1999. http://www.eric.ed.gov/ERICDocs/data/ericdocs2sql/content_storage_01/0000019b/80/17/a6/09.pdf

Chapter Six:
Tools for Students in the Digital Classroom

Poll Everywhere. http://www.polleverywhere.com/. Accessed 12/1/09

Chapter Seven:
Creating a Globalized Classroom

EPals. http://www.epals.com. Accessed: 12/03/09.

RezEd. http://www.rezed.org. Accessed: 08/08/09.

"Teenagers 'Spend an Average of 31 Hours Online." (2009). *Telegraph.* http://www.telegraph.co.uk/technology/4574792/Teenagers-spend-an-average-of-31-hours-online.html. Accessed: 12/02/09.

Wide Angle. PBS Broadcasting. http://www.pbs.org/wnet/wideangle/classroom/index.html. Accessed:12/03/09.

Chapter Eight:
Tools for the Teacher in the Digital Classroom

English Companion Ning. http://englishcompanion.ning.com. Accessed 6/18/09.

Open Office. http://www.openoffice.org. Accessed 8/24/09.

The Bookjam Ning. http://thebookjam.ning.com. Accessed 8/24/09.

Toondoo. http://www.toondoo.com. Accessed 10/4/09

Webspiration. http://www.mywebspiration.com. Accessed 10/4/09

Chapter Nine:
Teaching Individuality Through the Use Open Educational Resources

Applebaum, H. (1998). The American Work Ethic and The Changing Work Force. Retrieved from Google Books.

Atwell, G., & Pumilia, P. M. (2007). The new pedagogy of open content: bringing together production, knowledge, development, and learning [Electronic Version]. Data Science Journal, 6, S211-S219.

Brown, J. S., & Adler, R. P. (2008). Minds on fire: open education, the long tail, and learning 2.0 [Electronic Version]. Educause Review, 43, (1). Retrieved from EbscoHost.

Baraniuk, R.G. (2007). Challenges and opportunities for the open education movement:a connexions case study. Retrieved from Google Scholar.

Baraniuk, R.G. (2009). How open is open education? Domus. Retrieved from http://www.ece.rice.edu/~richb/OER-IP-Domus-mar09.pdf.

Chesbrough, H., Vanhaverbeke, W., & West, J. Open Innovation. Retrieved from Google Books.

Farber, R. (2009). Probing OER's huge potential [Electronic Version]. Scientific Computing, 26, (1), 29-29.

Iiyoshi, T., & Kumar, M. S. V. (Eds.). (2008). Opening Up Education. Boston: MIT Press.

Jensen, M. (2007). Authority 3.0: friend or foe to scholars? [Electronic Version].Journal of Scholarly Publishing, 39, (1). 33-43.

Peters, M., & Britez, R. (Eds.). (2008). Open Education and Education for Openness. Rotterdam: Sense Publishers.

Peters, M. (2009). Personalisation, personalised learning and the reform of social policy: the prospect of molecular governanace in the digitized society.

Ritzer, G. (2007). The Globalization of Nothing 2. Thousand Oaks: Pine Forge Press.

Rooper, T.G. (1902). Educational Studies and Addresses. Retrieved from Google Books.

Slabbert, J. (2006). Where is the post-modern truth we have lost in reductionist knowledge? [Electronic Version]. Journal of Curriculum Studies, 38, (6). 701-718.

Spring, J. (2007). A New Paradigm for Global School Systems. Mahwah: Lawrence Erlbaum Associates.

Winterman, D. (2007). Just another brick in the wall? BBC News Magazine Online. Retrieved from http://news.bbc.co.uk/1/hi/magazine/7021797.stm
.

Young, J. R. (2008). When professors print their own diplomas, who needs universities? [Electronic Version]. Chronicle of Higher Education, 55, (6). ¾

Zhao, Y. (2008). What knowledge has the most worth? The School Administrator. Retrieved from http://www.aasa.org/publications/saarticledetail.cfm?
ItemNumber=9737.

Chapter 10:
The Promise of OERs and the Inequalities that Exist

Baraniuk, Richard., & Burrus, C. Sidney. (2008). "Global Warming Toward Open Educational Resources." Communications of ACM. Vol. 58.9, 30-32. Retrieved 14.Feb.2009.

Digital divide. (2007). Retrieved from http://stats.oecd.org/glossary/detail.asp?ID=4719

Farber, Rob. (2009). "Probing OER's Huge Potential". Scientific Computing. Vol. 26.1, 29. Retrieved 14.Feb.2009.

Hole in the wall. (2006). Retrieved April 30, 2009, from Hole in Wall Education Ltd. Web site: http://www.hole-in-the-wall.com/

Iterating toward openness. (2006, February 3). The Current State of Open Educational Resources. Message posted to http://opencontent.org/blog/archives/247

Johnstone, Sally, M. "Open Educational Resources Serve the World". <u>Educause Quarterly</u>. http://net.educause.edu/ir/library/pdf/eqm0533.pdf

Kurshan, Barbara. "How Open-Source Curricula Could Bridge the Education Divide." <u>Connection: The Journal of the New England Board of Higher Education</u>. Vol. 21.4 (2007): 29-32. Retrieved 14.Feb.2009.

Lockette, T. (n.d.). Crossing the Gap. *Teaching Tolerance, 35*(Spring 2009). Retrieved February 16, 2009, from http://www.tolerance.org/teach/magazine/features.jsp?p=0&is=44&ar=1008

Lydersen, K. (2008, September 5). Boycott Underscores Disparities in Schools. *The Washington Post.* Retrieved February 5, 2009, from http://www.washingtonpost.com/wp-dyn/content/article/2008/09/04/AR2008090403398.html?hpid=sec-nation

One Laptop per Child. (2009, April 29). In *Wikipedia, The Free Encyclopedia*. Retrieved 14:28, April 30, 2009, from http://en.wikipedia.org/w/index.php?title=One_Laptop_per_Child&oldid=286905722

The hole in the wall project. (2002). Retrieved April 23, 2009, from PBS Frontline World Web site: http://www.pbs.org/frontlineworld/stories/india/thestory.html

Vadén, Tere and Suoranta, Juha. (2009). WikiWorld http://wikiworld.files.wordpress.com/2008/03/suoranta_vaden_wikiworld.pdf

Appendix:

Fatheree, J. (2009, July 17). Cell Phones in Education. Message posted to http://www.classroom20.com/group/CellPhonesinEducation

Imaginary City. http://kids.tate.org.uk/games/my-imaginary-city. Accessed 12/1/09

ReadWriteThink. http://www.readwritethink.org. Accessed 12/1/09.

Scratch. http://scratch.mit.edu/. Accessed 12/1/09.

The Book Report Sandwich Station. http://www.scholastic.com/kids/homework/sandwich.asp. Accessed 12/1/09.

About the Authors

Jeremy Rinkel is a published author and researcher in the fields of globalization, technology, and education. He believes that education is the key to solving world challenges. Before entering the field of education, he worked as Associate Director for Central IL Tourism, Marketing Director for Eagle Marketing, a business publication, and in advertising sales with the Effingham Daily News. At Central Illinois Tourism, he was responsible for strategic planning, as well as helping small communities develop tourism "action" plans. During his time in the business world, he noticed young people graduating without the communication, creativity, critical thinking, and collaboration skills needed to be successful in the world today. He currently teaches High School English and Speech and strives to use the most current technology and innovative teaching methods. He is studying Educational Policy with specialization in Globalization at the University of Illinois, Champaign-Urbana.

Majhon Phillips is a published scholar and researcher in the fields of globalization, youth education and sub-cultures. She has worked extensively with the use of technology in her Music and Language classrooms, as well as private lessons for over 5 years. Her students have been recognized as young scholars and presenters by multiple organizations including Modern Woodmen of America and the National Pre-Teen America Association. She is currently the President of Globalize Our Generation, Inc., an online after-school organization based around the ideas of teaching critical thinking and creativity to youths. She hopes to spread the use of technology, open education, and globalization through her work with this company. She is currently pursuing her PhD in Educational Policy Studies at the University of Illinois, Champaign-Urbana.

www.ingramcontent.com/pod-product-compliance
Lightning Source LLC
Chambersburg PA
CBHW062209080426
42734CB00010B/1853